THE BHS TRAINING MANUAL FOR THE

PTT

Incorporating the UKCC Level 2

NOTES FOR STUDENTS

This training manual provides a comprehensive guide to the techniques, knowledge and understanding required to prepare for the BHS PTT examination.

The
British
Horse
Society

THE BHS TRAINING MANUAL FOR THE

PTT

Incorporating the UKCC Level 2

Islay Auty FBHS

Updated and expanded by
Margaret Linington-Payne MA (Ed) BHSI

KENILWORTH PRESS

Copyright © 2013 The British Horse Society

First published in the UK in 2005 by Kenilworth Press, an imprint of Quiller Publishing Ltd

Updated edition published 2009
This edition published 2013

British Library Cataloguing-in-Publication Data
   A catalogue record for this book
   is available from the British Library

ISBN 978 1 905693 87 0

Line drawings by Dianne Breeze
Cover and book design by Sharyn Troughton
Printed in England by Ashford Colour Press Ltd

Kenilworth Press
An imprint of Quiller Publishing
Wykey House, Wykey, Shrewsbury, SY4 1JA
Tel: 01939 261616 Fax: 01939 261606
E-mail: info@quillerbooks.com
Website: www.kenilworthpress.co.uk

Contents

Picture Acknowledgements

All line drawings are by Dianne Breeze.

Picture sources

The author and publishers wish to acknowledge the following books as sources for the illustrations:

- *The BHS Complete Manual of Equitation*, Consultant Editor Patrick Print OBE FBHS, published by Kenilworth Press

- *Learn to Ride with the BHS*, by Islay Auty FBHS, published by Kenilworth Press

- *The BHS Instructors' Manual for Teaching Riding*, by Islay Auty FBHS, published by Kenilworth Press

How to Use this Book

The aim of this book is to provide students working towards the Preliminary Teaching Test with detailed guidance on how to prepare thoroughly for the examination and how to achieve UKCC Level 2 should they wish to do so.

You will find that the book echoes the structure of the syllabus and follows a clear pattern. There is information on 'What the assessor is looking for', followed by advice on 'How to become competent'.

It is important to realise that you can never achieve competence purely by reading a book, or indeed any number of books. Books can enhance and assist you in your study, but teaching riding is a very practical subject. It is up to you to ensure that your competence develops from practical experience, through observing lessons given by well-qualified or experienced teachers, and by developing your own practical teaching skills in as many controlled supervised situations as you can.

Understanding the PTT Exam

You will by now have had some experience of taking exams yourself, either through Pony Club tests, in taking your BHS Stage 1 and 2, or NVQ assessment and verification, but the PTT is likely to be the first time that you are assessed as a teacher.

It is therefore helpful during your training if you have had some genuine experience of riders who are novices or even complete beginners. You can gain this experience in the following ways:

- By observation in a commercial riding school of weekly riders of different ages and abilities.

- By leading novice children or adults in lessons under the supervision of a qualified coach. This could be done in association with a commercial riding school.

- By helping novice or beginner riders to lead their horses to the school, adjusting stirrups and girths and helping them again at the end of a lesson.

- By watching as many lessons as you can, given by more experienced coaches.

- By taking your generic BHS UKCC Level 1 endorsed qualification.

These opportunities allow you to appreciate just how limited the complete beginner's experience might be. It should help you to remember never to assume that a rider knows something already and to ensure that you teach every aspect of a lesson.

Study the syllabus carefully and discuss with your trainer where your weak areas might be, as well as your strengths. Make a plan for developing confidence and competence in the areas where you feel less secure. For example, if you feel nervous standing up and giving a short presentation, make sure that you take every opportunity to practise this by talking to groups of friends, family or informal gatherings so that you develop confidence. Confidence comes with practice and learning to teach takes time and practice.

You must feel confident about:

- Projecting your own voice from the start of the lesson.

- Teach according to what is happening in front of you, not to a stereotyped plan which may not apply to the pupils you have.

- Adhering to clear basic principles such as good basic position, application of the aids and control and understanding of the horse.

- Progressing the lesson in the way you believe is in the best interests of the class or individual, not because you think the assessors want to see you do something particular.

Your own presentation is important because it will give you an air of authority and image, which is important for an instructor/coach.

- Make sure that you have a hat, whip and gloves close by so that in extreme cases you could ride a pupil's horse that was behaving badly. If you teach in your hat the chin strap may be undone so that you can speak easily. It is not necessary to carry a stick while teaching.

- Dress as for previous exams (beige or fawn breeches, boots, shirt and tie and hacking jacket, have top coat or waterproof in case it is either cold or wet).

- Your image should be neat, tidy and professional.

The assessor will be looking for competence in teaching correct basic principles. You must be able to:

- Demonstrate self-confidence.

- Show an ability to project your voice both indoors and outside, and maintain an audible voice throughout.

- Control your riders.

- Develop a rapport with your riders and encourage them to think for themselves and give you feedback.

- Progress your pupils to some benefit and improvement.

Typical exam turnout – neat, tidy and professional.

- Deal with simple situations as they arise (e.g. if a horse is apparently lame, you must comment on it; if a rider appears worried, you must attempt to address the problem).

- You must demonstrate a competence to discuss basic lesson plans for a variety of teaching situations.

If at any stage the assessor feels that you are drifting away from developing your lesson satisfactorily, then he or she may suggest that you take a certain path (e.g. introduce jumping position if you are giving a jump lesson and have spent rather too long on the flat). Always regard this as a help, not an interference – the assessor is aiming to help you to show your best and is usually more aware of the time limitations of the exam than you are.

On arrival at the exam centre for your Preliminary Teaching Test, you will be briefed by the chief assessor, who will introduce the team of assessors for the day. The day's events will be explained to you and there will be a programme clearly listed for your benefit. The chief assessor will give each candidate a piece of paper on which there will be:

- A number.

- A subject for your class lesson (which will either be a lesson on the flat or one involving poles or jumps).

- A subject for your presentation.

- Whether you are required to give a lead-rein or a lunge lesson.

The PTT now consists of six units which can be taken altogether, individually or in any format that suits you.

The result sheet will be sent to you a few days after taking the exam and, if you have been successful, you will receive a certificate of achievement as well.

When you register for your PTT you will have the opportunity to also register for your United Kingdom Coaching Certificate (UKCC) Level 2 endorsement. The UKCC is a government initiative to introduce a standardised coaching qualification across all sports in the UK. Sportscoach UK (SCUK) is responsible for this, and the British Equestrian Federation (BEF) works with SCUK to ensure its delivery across all the BEF member bodies. Equestrian Qualifications GB (the new name for the awarding body arm of the BHS) is responsible for awarding the qualification.

To achieve the BHS Generic UKCC Level 2 you will have to top up your PTT qualification by completing a portfolio.

TIMETABLE/PROGRAMME

PRELIMINARY TEACHING TEST

08.15		Candidates assemble

Please have your membership card ready in order that the Assessors can check your identity

08.30		Candidates briefing
09.00	1-2	Class lesson
09.00	6-10	TU3 - Supporting participant(s') lifestyle through coaching sport Presentations and assessment of presentation work
09.30		Finish lesson
09.40	3-4	Class lesson (as above)
10.00	6-10	Break
10.10	7-10	TU4 - Understanding the principles of safe and equitable coaching practice Complete marking of presentation work if necessary
10.20	5-6	Class lesson (as above)
11.00	1-5	TU3 - Supporting participant(s') lifestyle through coaching sport Presentations and assessment of presentation work
11.00-11.20		Break for class lessons only
11.20	7-8	Class lesson (as above)
12.00	9-10	Class lesson (as above)
12.10	1-6	TU4 - Understanding the principles of safe and equitable coaching practice Complete marking of presentation work if necessary
12.40	1-6	Break
12.40-13.00		Teaching assessors bring all paperwork up to date
13.00		**LUNCH**
13.45	1-6	Lunge novice adult OR lead-rein lesson for a beginner
13.45	7-10	TU1 - Understanding the fundamentals of coaching sport TU2 - Understanding how to develop participant(s) through coaching sport
15.00	1-6	TU1 - Understanding the fundamentals of coaching sport TU2 - Understanding how to develop participant(s) through coaching sport
15.15	7-10	Lunge novice adult (two riders) OR lead-rein lesson for a beginner
16.15	7-10	Review with Assessors
16.30	1-6	Review with Assessors
16.50		EXAM ENDS - results sent by post. Assessors complete paperwork

PTT

EQL Level 3 Certificate in BHS Preliminary Teaching of Horse Riding

IMPORTANT: Candidates are advised to check that they are working from the latest examination syllabus, as examination content and procedure are liable to alteration. Contact the BHS Examinations Office for up-to-date information regarding the syllabus.

Syllabus

Candidates must show that they have the required qualities, and can apply the basic principles of teaching, e.g. manner, voice, control, etc. and that they have the ability to improve their pupils' horsemanship and horsemastership using a progressive plan. They must know the safety procedures and principles involved in the organisation of a lesson or hack (in the open country or on roads). They will be required to give a class lesson, which may include poles/jumps, a lunge or lead-rein lesson, and a presentation.

It is important that the candidates work to involve the learners in the activities and build up a good rapport. Learners must be engaged and take an active part in the sessions. Candidates will also join in discussions and answer questions on various topics as detailed in the syllabus.

They must have knowledge of how to proceed should there be an accident or an emergency and have sound knowledge of road safety.

N.B. Candidates may be required to give these lessons in the open and/or in a covered school. Ground poles or small jumps may be incorporated into the class lessons.

CLASS LESSON
Coach a Group of Riders for Improvement
11 credits/70 guided learning hours

Unit purpose and aims
The purpose of this unit is to coach a group of riders for improvement. The coach will be able to plan, deliver and evaluate the coaching session. The coach will create a positive and safe environment in which learning can take place. Candidates will be seen to coach either a session on the flat or a session over fences up to 2'6''. Candidates will be expected to coach up to Level 2 standard for riding on the flat or over fences.

Learner Outcomes		Assessment Criteria	
The learner will:		The learner can:	
1.	Be able to coach safely and efficiently	1.1	Use safe procedures to maintain health, safety and welfare of self, others and horses at all times
		1.2	Use time efficiently
2.	Be able to produce a session plan	2.1	Produce and adapt a pre prepared session plan
3.	Be able to prepare the coaching environment	3.1	Ensure the coaching environment is safe for use
		3.2	Ensure sufficient coaching resources are available
		3.3	Check horse and rider equipment is safe for use
4.	Be able to assess a group of riders	4.1	Outline the format of the coaching session to the riders
		4.2	Use exercises to assess horse and rider combinations
		4.3	Identify and evaluate riders strengths and weaknesses
		4.4	Discuss the suitability of proposed session plan with the Assessor
5.	Be able to coach a group of riders for improvement	5.1	Implement session plan as discussed
		5.2	Evaluate and assess the riders' positions and implement exercises to facilitate improvement
		5.3	Evaluate and assess the riders' use of natural and artificial aids and implement exercises to facilitate improvement
		5.4	Communicate technically correct explanations
		5.5	Establish a rapport with the riders and obtain feedback to facilitate learning
		5.6	Use their voice and body language to good effect
6.	Be able to evaluate the coaching session	6.1	Provide feedback to the riders at the end of the coaching session
		6.2	Give an action plan to the riders for their development
		6.3	Reflect on and evaluate personal performance
		6.4	Devise an action plan to develop personal coaching practice

INDIVIDUAL LESSON
Coach an Inexperienced Rider for Improvement
8 credits/50 guided learning hours

Unit purpose and aims
The purpose of this unit is to coach an inexperienced rider for improvement. The coach will be able to plan, deliver and evaluate the coaching session. The coach will create a positive and safe environment in which learning can take place. Candidates will be seen to coach either a session on the lunge or the lead rein.

Learner Outcomes		Assessment Criteria	
The learner will:		The learner can:	
1.	Be able to coach safely and efficiently	1.1	Use safe procedures to maintain health, safety and welfare of self, others and horses at all times
		1.2	Use time efficiently
2.	Be able to produce a session plan	2.1	Produce and adapt a pre prepared session plan
3.	Be able to prepare the coaching environment	3.1	Ensure the coaching environment is safe for use
		3.2	Ensure sufficient coaching resources are available
		3.3	Check horse and rider equipment is safe for use
4.	Be able to assess an inexperienced rider	4.1	Outline the format of the coaching session to the rider
		4.2	Use exercises to assess horse and rider combination
		4.3	Identify and evaluate rider's strengths and weaknesses
		4.4	Discuss the suitability of proposed session plan with the Assessor
5.	Be able to coach an inexperienced rider for improvement	5.1	Implement session plan as discussed
		5.2	Evaluate and assess the rider's position and implement exercises to facilitate improvement
		5.3	Evaluate and assess the rider's use of natural aids and implement exercises to facilitate improvement
		5.4	Communicate technically correct explanations
		5.5	Establish a rapport with the rider and obtain feedback to facilitate learning
		5.6	Use their voice and body language to good effect
6.	Be able to evaluate the coaching session	6.1	Provide feedback to the rider at the end of the coaching session
		6.2	Give an action plan to the rider for their development
		6.3	Reflect on and evaluate personal performance
		6.4	Devise an action plan to develop personal coaching practice

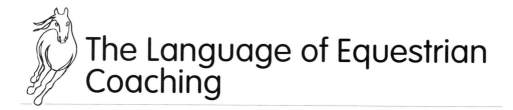

The Language of Equestrian Coaching

If you have been having regular instruction you will probably be aware of the terminology that is in general use for helping to keep the ride safe and under control. If you are coaching an individual with whom you have a good rapport and working relationship this terminology may appear too formal and unnecessary. It is very useful to be confident using the terminology because most riders will understand what is meant and, when working as a ride, will expect it.

- Working as a ride following each other is called working in closed order.

- Working as individuals within a group is called working in open order.

When asking all the riders to undertake an exercise together:

- 'Whole ride preparing to (e.g. go forward into working trot rising)'. Then pause to give the riders time to prepare themselves and their horses for the task. Then say 'Whole ride…trot'.

Example 2. (Asking the ride to undertake a figure when all are trotting)

- 'Whole ride twenty metre circle at A and then go large'.

When giving a command to undertake a task at a certain letter you must time the command so that the riders are able to prepare themselves and their horses and perform a smooth exercise.

When asking the riders to undertake an individual exercise with the rider in front going first the command 'Leading files in succession' is used. For example when asking each rider to canter one at a time to the rear of the ride:

- 'Leading files in succession prepare to go forward into working trot and at the next suitable corner pick up canter and canter to the rear of the ride'.

You should then ask the riders if they all understand what they have to do. You may point out the safety factors and that they must trot well before the rear file, or if they are unable to stop they should circle away. You then say 'Leading file commence the exercise'. Once they have finished you say 'Next commence' (or you could use their name which is more personal and friendly).

If you want the riders to undertake an exercise one at a time with the person at the rear going first you would use a similar sequence but use the term 'Rear files in succession...'

Always make sure commands are given in good enough time for the riders to prepare for whatever they are being asked to do. This will take practise. Listen to and watch experienced instructors/coaches to help understand how far in advance you need to prepare a group of riders to undertake an exercise successfully.

Rules of the School

It is important that you know the rules of the school and that the riders also understand those that are relevant to them.

The main rules are:

- Always knock and ask for permission to enter before going into a school or manége.

- When working as a ride always keep a safe distance from the horse in front.

- When working in open order:

  a) Always walk on an inner track, leaving the outer track free for those going at a faster pace.

  b) It is better to turn across the school to undertake a downwards transition so you do not interfere with horses behind you.

  c) Cross left hand to left hand with somebody working at the same pace as you.

  d) Give way to lateral work.

  e) Always be aware of what other riders are doing.

  f) Before leaving the school always inform other riders and ensure they have heard you.

UNIT 1
Class Lesson

Coach a Group of Riders for Improvement

11 Credits

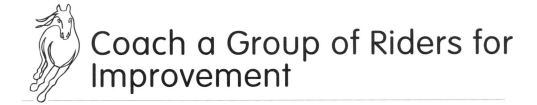# Coach a Group of Riders for Improvement

Lesson Topics – flat and jump

Candidates will need to prepare lesson plans for all eight class lesson topics detailed below and lesson plans for an open brief for a flat and a jump lesson prior to the exam day.

Class flat lesson topics:

1. Assess your riders' ability to ride transitions and teach them to improve their transition work. Ensure their basic position is maintained in halt, walk, trot and canter.

2. Assess your riders' ability and teach them to improve their position on the flat using appropriate exercises and movements, including work without stirrups.

3. Assess your riders' ability and, using appropriate exercises, work to improve their co-ordination and application of the aids, including exercises, corners, straight lines and changes of rein and school figures.

4. Assess your riders' ability and work to improve their feel for rhythm and balance using appropriate exercises and movements, including circles and serpentines to improve lateral bend.

Class jump lessons topics:

5. Assess your riders' jump position and work using ground poles and a fence. Then use appropriate exercises to improve the rhythm, balance and co-ordination.

6. Assess your riders' ability over a single fence and progress to using a grid of fences to improve your riders' position and feel.

7. Assess your riders' ability over a single fence and then use several combination/related distance fences to improve their position and feel. Use canter approaches and changes of direction.

8. Assess your riders' ability over a single fence and then work to improve their work through combinations and related distances with the emphasis on working in canter.

Open brief for flat and jump lessons:

This is a plan for a lesson the candidate feels would be suitable for riders they have not assessed before. The plan may list a selection of exercises that could be used up to Stage 2 level riders. The candidate should then select those exercises that are relevant to the riders and, as with any lesson plan, this may need adjusting on the exam day, depending on the type of riders, horses and how they progress.

What the assessor is looking for

- You should present a neat image with a clean, tidy, professional turnout, and from the outset you must convey confidence in both your voice and body language.

- You should come with all your lesson plans prepared so you do not have to worry about these.

Correct riding position – shoulder, hip and heel aligned.

A typical novice rider position, as yet showing no depth.

- Your voice must be positive and audible throughout the lesson. Remember to project your voice with clear words that are not hurried. Position the ride near to the assessor when you are talking to your pupils, so that the assessor can hear too.

- It is likely that your riders will be mounted and waiting for you in a line. Introduce yourself and find out your riders' names and check their tack. Ask your riders if there is anything specific they would like to work on as individuals. Also ask if they need help with either their reins or stirrups and suggest they check their girths. Find out if the riders are all mounted on horses they have ridden before.

- Discuss what you have been asked to teach, so that your pupils know the subject matter or aims of the lesson that you will give.

- Demonstrate confidence and ability in your control of the ride as you start to work with them. It does not matter if you choose to work the ride in closed order or in open order so long as you have clearly directed the ride in what they are to do and you are sure that they both understand and can carry out your instructions.

- Choose work that shows you know how to assess riders and progress the work to a logical plan.

Rider faults: rounded shoulders, stiff arms, over-short reins, rounded back.

Rider faults: sitting behind the movement, reins too long, and lower leg forward.

- Be able to identify where riders have faults and weaknesses and be able to offer assistance for improvement.

- Once you have assessed the riders the assessor will discuss with you how you feel the lesson will progress and whether the lesson plan needs to be adapted.

- Show confidence in choosing work that will address the riders' faults and help to improve them.

- Choose school figures that help to develop the riders' competence and feel for the horses, from which you can make suitable corrections of position faults or aid application.

- Frequently encourage the riders to feed back to you by asking them questions that will make them think about what they are doing.

- With a jumping lesson, the handling of the equipment that you need (poles, jump wings, cups, etc.) must be done with proficiency and competence, through familiarity and awareness of where to place the equipment with regard to maintaining the safety of your ride.

- Ideally, in an exam you will have someone to assist you so that the equipment can be moved into place for you to use without reducing your valuable teaching time.

- You must inform your helper where the poles/jumps are to be placed and you must always check yourself that the jump and any pole distances have been placed or measured to your satisfaction.

- Spare equipment should be stacked neatly out of the way of the ride's activity, with special awareness of keeping jump cups tidy and safe. Jump cups must never be left on a wing if they are not holding a pole.

- You must assess the ride with particular emphasis on the lesson being a jumping lesson. It would therefore be wise to ensure that the riders are riding with stirrups at jumping length before you start. Probably see them in walk, trot and canter and ask them to take 'light seat' at some stage of this initial work.

- Once you have assessed the ride the assessor will discuss with you how you feel the lesson will progress and whether the lesson plan will be adapted.

- You must be able to recognise when the rider is in good balance in the jumping position.

- You must also be able to identify the area(s) of fault with the riders' positions and be able to suggest help to assist in improvement.

- You must be able to recognise if faults are arising from poor balance or incorrect position, or from poor understanding of the use of correct aids or their application.

- If aid application is the problem, then relevant help must be forthcoming once you have identified the weak area.

- Your choice of work will be directed by your initial assessment and also to some degree by the 'brief' you are given for your lesson. The 'brief' is a broad-based subject around which you should be structuring your lesson plan.

- Whatever you choose for your lesson, you must use appropriate distances between your poles and safely constructed jumps according to the ability of your horses and riders.

Rider showing a 'light seat' or jumping position
(also known as forward seat or poised position).

- At the end of the lesson be confident about talking to the group as a whole (briefly) and then individually. Provide some clear ideas for further improvement by giving the riders something to be working on in the coming days or weeks after the lesson.

- The assessor will then discuss the lesson and riders with you. You should reflect on the lesson truthfully, pointing out what went well, what could have gone better and how you could have improved it. The assessor will discuss this with you. He/she will also obtain feedback from the riders.

How to become competent

- You will be required to teach a group of three or four riders for approximately 30 minutes. The riders should be able to walk, trot and canter and jump small fences. The lesson will probably take place in a 20m x 40m school which may be indoors or outside.

- Practise remembering names, as it is important to be involved with your riders and forgetting their names does not promote this feeling. If you find it difficult to remember names then take a small notebook or postcard with you to jot down names so that a glance down will remind you (e.g. Sarah – bay horse with martingale; John – brown horse, white brushing boots).

- With any riders for whom you are responsible, remind them to check their girths before you move off and again after five or ten minutes' riding. Be able to adjust stirrups for your riders and/or advise on level stirrups.

- It is important for safety reasons to ask the riders if they have ridden the horse before, and have they checked their girths and stirrups?

- An initial assessment of the group is vital (it allows you to decide how the work should progress). This assessment might involve some walk, trot and canter with a change of direction.

- During this assessment, while maybe not yet fully 'teaching' your pupils, nevertheless you should communicate with them, beginning to introduce some strengths and weaknesses in the riders. It is acceptable to work the ride in closed or open order as long as you explain clearly which you are choosing and why. If

VARIOUS WAYS TO CHANGE THE REIN

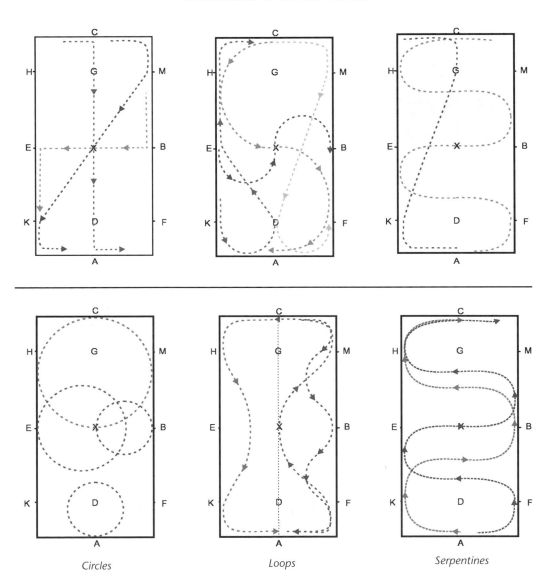

Circles	*Loops*	*Serpentines*

As a coach, you have a vast number of school figures to choose from when planning exercises. Know them well, and, as important, know how to teach them accurately.

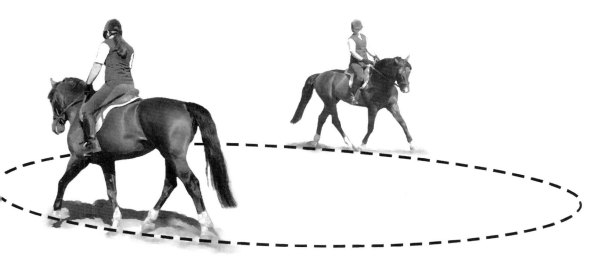

Riding a circle. Teach your riders the aids that create this figure: inside rein indicating direction; inside leg on the girth for energy, motivating the inside hind leg; outside rein controlling the pace and bend; and outside leg controlling the hindquarters, slightly behind the girth.

you choose open order you must check the riders are used to this and understand the rules of the school.

- With fairly inexperienced riders it is often easier to assess them in closed order rather than have fairly novice riders you have never taught before in open order.

- In the first few minutes learn to assess the basic competence and control of each rider, the basic position, whether they are 'leaders' or 'followers'.

- Choose simple straightforward exercises to start with, going large, 20m circles and changes of rein across the diagonal.

- You must be able to assess each rider's correct basic position and to decide, if there are faults, from where they originate. (E.g. a loose position may be caused by the rider trying to ride with overlong stirrups. Heels drawing up may be caused by the rider gripping with the lower leg and thus drawing the heel up.)

- Watch as many class lessons as you can so that you see riders' positions and faults and what other instructors do to improve them.

- Understand the value of working riders without stirrups (in walk, trot and/or canter) to develop the depth and effect of the rider's position.

- Choose work that will not overtire your riders or be beyond their ability, which then may cause a loss of confidence and compromise safety.

- You must talk to your riders to find out their knowledge and obtain feedback to fully understand what they are feeling and thinking.

- It is important that the riders understand the aids for basic exercises (e.g. turns, circles, simple changes of pace and direction).

- It is your responsibility to maintain safety in the lesson at all times and to the best of your ability. You must therefore make clear judgements about what to do and when to do it. This is always dependent on the circumstances 'on that day'.

- Always teach what you see in front of you and what is actually happening. Never teach a lesson that you think the assessor might want to see, or that the rider chooses, despite your being doubtful about the rider's competence.

- Development of the work is essential for maintaining enthusiasm and motivating riders towards further achievement.

- Repetition is essential for ensuring that your riders become competent.

- By watching other teachers you will develop a range of exercises, movements and work that will provide the repetition for riders, while also introducing variety to maintain interest.

- As a preliminary teacher never assume knowledge. Even if a rider tells you that he or she can canter or jump you must always make your own assessment and progress the work in accordance with your judgement.

- Never pressurise a rider into attempting to do something that they tell you they cannot or do not want to do.

- Always have your full attention on your rider(s). Do not be distracted by anything or anyone who disturbs the lesson.

- Whenever possible, riders should be of similar standard in a lesson. Progress should be directed by the least competent rider in the group.

- Learn to be aware of outside influences which might have a disrupting effect on your class lesson (e.g. horses turned out in a field, galloping about / noisy vehicle outside the school). Awareness can allow you to adapt the lesson content (e.g. come back to walk if working in trot or canter) so that safety is maintained before control is lost.

- Make sure that you understand the basis of the rider being able to ride the horse forward from leg to hand and that the security of the rider's position dictates their ability to apply clear and coordinated aids.

- Practise projecting your voice with confidence throughout the lesson. Clearly expressed words can then be easily heard and will not be lost into the surface or into the wind if outside.

- For any lesson of any level you must be confident, and confidence only comes from experience and feeling comfortable and familiar with what you are doing.

- Watch as many jumping lessons as you can, given by more experienced instructors.

- Go to jumping competitions and watch riders competing.

- Become very familiar with how jumps are built, from a simple cross pole to a more demanding double on one or two non-jumping strides, to a vertical fence and an oxer.

- Help more experienced jumping teachers while they teach, but be in the school and help them move fences and put down poles, so that you develop an awareness of how quickly and efficiently you must learn to use the equipment.

- Learn to keep your eyes constantly on your riders; even if you are moving poles with your feet, or adjusting the height of a fence, you must keep watching your riders.

- Never allow a rider to approach a fence if you do not have your eyes on them – and preferably your full attention as well.

Working in jumping position over a single pole and several poles.

- Occasionally, you may still be speaking to a rider who has just completed an exercise but you must be looking at the rider who is starting to negotiate the fence or poles.

- In the early stages of your teaching you may need to have only one rider moving around at a time so you do not have too much to concentrate on. As you develop in competence it is acceptable and practical to have the riders working in open order and over poles using their judgement to maintain space from each other.

- Awareness is vital, you must be able to develop a 'feel' for when a horse is getting a little sharp and may start to rush a jump, or when a rider is getting nervous and starting to 'hold back' restricting the forwardness to a jump.

- Watch more senior coaches working with different riders through grids and jumping exercises.

- You must learn basic distances for jumping but ultimately it is how you 'teach' the rider that dictates whether the distance works for that horse or rider or not.

- Take basic distances such as: trotting pole distance at 4ft 6in (1.35m) apart; a placing pole to a small fence taken from trot at approx 9ft (2.7m); a trot approach to a small fence followed by one non-jumping stride to a second fence on 18ft (5.4m); and the same two fences with a canter approach 21ft (6.3m). These distances would be acceptable for a basic jumping lesson with rhythmical reasonable forward paces. However, the teacher must be able to help adjust the approach if necessary if a distance is riding too long or short, rather than just identifying the distance as being 'wrong'.

- A basic ability to 'see' whether a distance suits a horse and rider or not is essential at this level. This must be learned through 'feel', awareness and discussion with a more senior instructor who will help you to see what they are seeing and aware of.

- Carefully consider the use of a placing pole to a fence. Some horses may rush, others may lose rhythm, others it may help.

- You must teach some basic jumping lessons, use poles regularly and feel familiar with moving poles around and recognising when the poles have been rolled out of place.

- Learn to work in a tidy, safe environment and always move spare poles into a tidy stack out of the way of the working ride.

- Always take cups out of stands if they are not holding a pole.

- Always keep spare cups tucked under the sides of wings or in the spare stack of jumps or in a designated receptacle.

- Collapsable cups should be used for the back rail of a spread fence.

- If in doubt always check a distance if you think it has been moved or is inappropriate, telling a rider to wait before approaching a fence.

- Always choose exercises and fences that are well within the range of ability of your riders.

- Be able to discuss what future work you might do with riders on another occasion. Never rush to build an extra fence or another element to a grid when that might compromise safety. Discuss the option of putting in another fence or part to a grid as a possibility for a future lesson.

• Be prepared to talk truthfully about how the lesson went, and to give your thoughts and feelings about it. Reflecting on what you have done is important. If you are unable to realise what has gone well and what has not, then it is difficult for you to improve your coaching methods. Remember, nobody is perfect and we can always improve by approaching something a different way, or by spotting problems earlier, or by choosing different exercises to help riders.

UNIT 2
Individual Lesson
Coach an Inexperienced Rider for Improvement

8 Credits

Coach an Inexperienced Rider for Improvement

- The individual lesson lasts approximately 25 minutes in total. You will be given a brief that is relevant to the rider you are given. It will probably involve asking you to assess the rider and work to improve their position. The rider may be a child or an adult, and they should be of a beginner/novice standard. The lesson will be either a lunge or a lead-rein lesson.

- For the lunge and lead-rein lesson come to the exam with a generic lesson plan which you will be able to adapt on the day.

The lunge lesson:

- You should introduce yourself to the rider and ask them their name and to tell you how much riding they have done. Ask them if they have any particular issues they would like to work on and what their long-term goals are. Then ask them to stand in a safe place within the school (possibly a corner, or if the school is divided by poles, then outside the pole area).

- The horse will have been warmed up for you so it will be necessary only to ensure that he is responsive to your aids. Briefly check the tack and if you have any issues discuss these with your assessor. Send the horse out onto one rein (most people send the horse out onto the left rein first, so this may be advisable as he may be expecting that). Lunge him for a few circles asking for one or two trot/walk/trot transitions. Be positive so that you quickly take command of the situation. Do not forget your rider in the corner – if this were a real lesson they would be paying for your time. Perhaps discuss the number of beats in walk and trot with them or talk about the benefits of lungeing. Change the rein, attach the side-reins and try the horse briefly on the other rein. If you feel there are any issues with regard to using this horse for a novice lunge lesson then talk to the assessor about it. This assessment should take no more than a few minutes.

- Stop the horse, unclip the side reins, untwist the reins, check the girth and then mount your rider. Make sure that the rider uses a correct technique for mounting. They can mount from a mounting block if you feel that is advisable. Remember, mounting from a block is easier for the horse as well as the rider. Ensure that the rider checks the stirrup length before they mount and, although you must check the girth, encourage them to get into the habit of also checking it themselves. When your rider mounts, assist as necessary and check their technique. See that they have turned the stirrup the right way and that the reins are correctly held. During all this you must have control of the horse, and your whip should be safely tucked under your arm with the lash end of the whip pointing towards the ground and the lash behind you.

- Once the rider is mounted check that their stirrups are level and do not forget to attach the horse's side-reins. Assess the rider briefly on both reins and decide where their positional issues lie.

- You may then have an opportunity to discuss your proposed lesson plan with the assessor. Be honest about your rider and tell the assessor what you feel about their position, confidence and ability and put forward your ideas as to what you are going to do. Remember the rider will hear this, so be polite about them and always say something positive first.

- The main body of the lesson is working to improve the rider. The exercises you choose must be relevant to the rider's issues. It is no use giving arm-circling exercises when the rider is very stiff in the hips. A lot of beginner and novice riders are very tight through their hips. This can be partly due to nerves and partly due to general stiffness through the joints. Always work to get the rider central in the saddle with the two imaginary straight lines running ear–shoulder–hip–heel and elbow–arm–reins–bit rings.

- Your rider may well need to hold the neck strap or pommel to help maintain their balance. This should be encouraged. They will feel safer and then relax into their position more.

- A rider who sits in an armchair position needs to be encouraged to sit up. Riding briefly with one hand in the small of the back will help to give them the feel of sitting on their seat bones. Holding a hand in that position can be very tiring (as can any exercise that the rider is not used to) so make sure you do not overstress the rider. Standing in the stirrups (holding the neck strap at halt in the first

Lungeing the rider without stirrups to improve position, depth and security.

instance) can also encourage an armchair rider to come more into balance. A rider who is very behind the movement may well have their stirrups too short. Riding without stirrups is excellent to help lengthen the rider's legs and generally improve balance and position. You must assess whether you think the rider is secure enough to ride without stirrups.

- There is no set rule as to whether or not you take away the reins or stirrups from the rider. You must assess whether doing either will help the rider to improve. When coaching in a known environment with a known client you may well take away the reins and stirrups at the same time. However, in an exam situation, with a rider and a horse you do not know, it may be advisable to take away just one thing at a time if you feel doing so could benefit the rider.

- During the session it is important to keep your rider involved. Ask frequently for feedback about how what they are doing feels and if they can feel any difference in their position. Depending on the experience of the rider you can also ask them about the feel they are getting from the horse itself. Do not just bark orders at them all the time. Ask them about how their body feels and how tired it is becoming. Allow them time to give you feedback and make sure you react to it.

Stirrup leathers snugly and securely crossed over the withers so that the rider can work comfortably without stirrups.

- At the end of the session bring the horse to a halt, walk to the horse and undo the side-reins. Talk to the rider about their strengths and weaknesses and give them some things to work on during their next session. Dismount the rider safely and make sure they run up their stirrups.

- The assessor will then approach you to discuss the session. Think carefully about what has happened and identify the positives. If you feel there is anything that could have been undertaken differently then discuss this also. Self-reflection is an important part of coaching – unless we think about what we have done and how we have done it, it will be very difficult to improve ourselves.

- The assessor will ask the rider to give very briefly one or two thoughts on the session. As long as you have built up a good rapport, involved the rider and used exercises that are relevant you should not worry about this at all.

- Many coaches seem to spend a great deal of time making the rider undertake arm- and leg-circling exercises. If these are relevant to the rider's issues then you will not be penalised, but if they are just being used to 'fill up' the lesson time you will be marked down.

- There are many useful exercises you can use to help improve a rider's position (see next section). In an exam it is always best to ask the rider to undertake any exercises initially at halt. This will be easier for them and you can assess the reaction of the horse.

- It is absolutely vital that you pay attention to safety throughout the session. It is no easy task to control a horse and give a lunge lesson at the same time. Your lungeing technique must be efficient and effective. It is possible to fail this section if you are not safe. A rider will not have confidence in you as a coach if you are inefficient and give the impression of uncertainty.

What the assessor is looking for

- The first thing the assessor will be looking for is a safe and established lungeing technique; without this you will be unable to give a competent lesson.

- Ensure that you are well practised in lungeing and you feel confident in lungeing unknown horses.

- It is essential that you are able to send the horse forward sufficiently in order to give a competent lesson.

- Mount the rider with the side-reins unclipped from the bit, clip up the side-reins and work the rider first with the reins and stirrups while you make an initial assessment.

- In this assessment, the assessor will want to see you make clear observations about the rider's position, noticing both the strengths and weaknesses.

- The lesson should be active and interesting. Be sure to make frequent changes of rein and work in an animated way with your pupil, making sure they are kept involved.

- Throughout the whole lesson you must demonstrate safety and awareness.

How to become competent

- I make no apology for repeating that there are no short cuts to competence. You must practise lungeing frequently and with as many different horses as possible.

- Your lungeing technique must be secure and consistent. Make sure that you can manage the rein and whip efficiently on both reins, without getting the rein muddled.

- Make sure that you have lunged a rider as often as possible; if you can, start with a pony (and child) which tends to be easier to manage, and then move to a horse and adult rider.

- Watch more experienced instructors giving lunge lessons and try to have a lesson or two yourself.

- Practise exercises yourself that might be useful to improve riders, feel the effect they have on your position and consider the value they have.

- Gradually develop a range of exercises which work different parts of the body and help the rider's balance and suppleness.

Suggested exercises for improving the softness of the hips and lower body:

- Asking the rider to bring their whole leg back from the hip.

- Lifting up the knees, turning them out and pushing legs down and back.

- With the hand hold the foot and draw the lower leg up so the leg is near to the cantle.

- Ankle circling.

- Standing up in the stirrups.

Suggested exercises for improving the softness of the upper body:

- Put chin to chest and then tilt the head back.

- Shoulder shrugs.

- Shoulder rolls.

- Turn head to look as far left as possible and then as far right as possible.

- Rotate the upper body left then right.

- Learn to lunge a horse briefly and then mount a rider quickly and efficiently so that you do not waste time in this process and can get on with your lesson.

- Time is always limited in an exam and the more proficient you can be in getting on with any lesson, the more experience you will demonstrate and the more time you will have to improve your pupil.

- Safety and awareness are paramount. If in doubt about how a horse might be behaving or reacting then be cautious before taking away reins or stirrups. If a horse is misbehaving at the other end of the school and your rider is without stirrups, give them back their stirrups as a precautionary measure and say why you are doing that.

- Show an ability to communicate with your pupils; knowing how they feel about the work you are doing, will help in their learning process.

- Your awareness of the correct basic riding position is always of prime importance. Make sure that you can recognise when a rider is sitting correctly or where they are out of balance and need help to adjust their position.

- Watch many riders and their positions and their balance and how this may change according to what they are trying to do with the horse or how the horse is going.

The lead-rein lesson:

- The lead-rein lesson will last 25 minutes in total. You will be given a brief that is relevant to the rider you have. It will probably involve assessing the rider and working to improve their position. The rider will either be a child or a beginner adult.

- Many people think that a lead-rein lesson is a 'soft option'. To give a good lead-rein lesson, however, is extremely difficult. To position yourself so you can build up a rapport with the rider, control the horse/pony and give a worthwhile lesson takes a great deal of practice. You need to be by the horse/pony's shoulder. You should not be in front of the horse/pony and 'drag' it along. You need to be able to look at the rider when you are talking to them to build up a rapport and ensure that what they are doing is correct, but you must also be aware of where you are going!

- Introduce yourself to the rider, ask their name and spend a short time talking to them to start to build up a rapport. Discuss what riding they have done and what their goals are. Ask them if they have ridden the horse/pony before and, if they have, what he is like. Check the tack. Make sure there is a neck strap and that the method given to you to lead the horse is safe.

- If the rider is a complete beginner you will have to teach them to mount. Make sure you are accurate in this. If they can ride a little then ensure they mount correctly. Using a mounting block is a good idea. It makes the task easier for both horse and rider. Pay particular attention to checking the girth and stirrup length before mounting. Try to get the rider into good habits right from the beginning by ensuring the reins and stirrups are not twisted and that the rider understands the horse has feelings.

- Once the rider is mounted make sure you check that the stirrups are of an equal length and they are sitting centrally.

- Spend a few minutes assessing the rider. Work on both reins and at the same time make sure you are taking responsibility for the control of the horse/pony. Decide on what the rider's issues are and how you can go about improving them. Then you may spend a few minutes discussing with the assessor what you are going to do and why. Remember: you will be in ear- shot of the rider, so be polite about them and point out the positives first.

- The main part of your lesson is how you work the rider to improve them. It is important that the exercises you use take the rider's age and previous experience into consideration. The exercises must be relevant to the rider. Safety must be the priority, but the lesson must be interesting and lively as well. If the rider is a complete beginner they may need to hold the neck strap or pommel for most of the work at the beginning of the session. Do not overface the rider with the exercises you choose. Children may well enjoy toe touching exercises at the halt, helping to make a weak lower leg secure, but a beginner adult may find this exercise difficult, and that does nothing to boost their confidence.

- If the rider is a complete beginner you may find yourself staying in walk the whole lesson. You may progress to a small amount of sitting trot. It is vital that you ask the rider to undertake work that will help to build confidence and competence and not just 'use up' the lesson time. If you feel it is relevant and safe to do so, you can do work without stirrups. Take time to engage the rider in conversation – a rider who is talking is breathing and therefore less stiff than one who is holding their breath. Get them to think about what they are doing and to tell you how it feels. All this will help with building a rapport and will ensure the rider enjoys themself as well as learns. It is vital that a child's lesson is fun, but that does not mean to say you should sacrifice their position or ability to improve for this.

- Change the rein frequently. There may well be another lead-rein lesson going on in the same area. Keep an eye out for what the other combination is doing so you do not get in each other's way. The assessor may well be moving around the area with you. They will not get in the way. They are just ensuring they hear what is being said, giving you every opportunity to show your abilities.

- If you feel the rider is competent in walk and trot you may wish to let them off the lead rein. It may be best at first to walk and trot them while you are holding the very end of the lead rein a short distance away from them, just to make sure they can cope. If you do let them off the lead rein, stay close to them.

- If there is time you may wish to use cones/blocks or poles for the rider to negotiate as an obstacle course. Even riding around a single cone can give a beginner rider a real challenge and create much discussion.

- Remember to be enthusiastic and show a real desire to keep your rider motivated. Whenever you teach you must really want your riders to improve, and this is just as true for a lead-rein lesson as for a class session.

- At the end of the session the assessor will give you an opportunity to reflect on the lesson. Be honest with yourself and the assessor. Do find the positives from the session, and if you feel there was anything you could have done differently then discuss it. The assessor may well question you on specific areas or engage in a general discussion about what they have seen. They will also briefly ask the rider for feedback on the session.

What the assessor is looking for

- It is essential with any novice or beginner rider that you are able to assess the person's basic balance when they first get onto the horse/pony. Some riders have a greater natural balance, confidence and ability to sit automatically in the optimum position on a horse than others. The naturally balanced, confident rider will tend to find more security from the start. You must show an ability to recognise the beginner or novice rider's innate ability.

- Be able to work out if the rider is insecure or unbalanced and know how to make adjustments which will help them adopt a more correct balanced position.

- You must show an ability to develop a good rapport with the rider, being tactful and encouraging. The rider must be involved.

- The age of the rider may be relevant to their level of confidence and understanding and to their attention span and this should be a consideration shown in the way you teach.

- The lesson must demonstrate safe practice at all times and should show a progression which is interesting and appropriate for the confidence and level of ability of the rider.

How to become competent

- If you can gain some genuine experience of giving lead-rein lessons or assisting in leading while another instructor is teaching, then this will be invaluable to you.

- Watch novice and beginner riders being taught by someone of more experience.

- Watch the inadequacies that the majority of beginners have when their only contact with the horse/pony may be for one hour per week.

- Remember that someone who is able to practise a skill daily or even several times a week will be much more proficient than someone who has only one hour each week to revisit their chosen activity.

- You must be constantly aware of the need to assist and repeat terms and actions which to you may be very familiar but to the novice or beginner rider are still quite alien.

- Be aware that it takes many repetitions of simple tasks to achieve even a basic level of competence, so do not worry that you may appear to be repeating things many times over.

- Try to develop a versatility in repeating the same task or information without confusing your rider. In this way you will keep lessons interesting while ensuring that sufficient repetition does convey competence gradually (e.g. In walk there are many changes of rein that could be used to encourage your rider to concentrate on the aids for turning).

- Make sure that you are competent in leading both ponies (for child riders) and horses (for adults) working evenly on both reins and being able to lead the animal efficiently, especially in trot, while still able to glance at your rider and make simple suggestions.

- You need to be physically fit enough to conduct a lesson on foot involving walk and trot and capably communicating with your pupil without getting breathless.

- If you are sharing the school with other lessons going on simultaneously make sure you use the school sensibly and with awareness of other instructors.

PTT
EQL Level 3
Theory Units

IMPORTANT: There are four theory units. Although they look very complicated when you read the assessment criteria they are assessed in a practical way and the information in the following pages relate to these units. Unit 3 is assessed via the presentation. There are five presentations that you need to prepare before attending the exam.

Syllabus

THEORY UNIT (TU) 1
Understanding the Fundamentals of Coaching Sport
3 credits/22 guided learning hours

Unit purpose and aims
This unit assesses the coach's understanding of their role in the planning, implementing, analysing and revising coaching sessions. They also will identify a range of methods of developing learning, performance and the effective management of participant behaviour.

Learner Outcomes	Assessment Criteria
The learner will:	The learner can:
1. Understand the role of a coach	1.1 Describe how to ensure that the participant is at the centre of the coaching process
	1.2 Explain how to empower participant(s)' choice, discovery of solutions and need to develop at their own pace
	1.3 Describe how to develop and maintain positive relationships with and between participant(s)
	1.4 Describe how to provide a coaching environment that motivates, recognises and values diversity, controls risk, encourages challenge, enjoyment and achievement
	1.5 Identify methods to develop participant(s)' confidence and self esteem
	1.6 Describe how to identify opportunities for the coach to reflect and develop their coaching practice
	1.7 List the different support personnel that can contribute to coaching sessions
	1.8 Describe how support personnel can be used to contribute to coaching sessions
	1.9 Explain the importance of positively promoting the role of officials in competition
	1.10 Define what is acceptable in terms of a coach:participant relationship
	1.11 Explain the consequences of not adhering to the principles of what is acceptable in terms of a coach:participant relationship
	1.12 Identify the components of a Code of Practice for coaching which allows high standards of personal conduct to be maintained and a positive image of the sport to be projected
	1.13 Outline the types of information that the coach should provide to participant(s) after a coaching session

2.	Understand the coaching process	2.1	Outline how to identify participant(s)' needs
		2.2	List the sources of information that a coach can use when planning and preparing coaching sessions
		2.3	Identify the types of information about participants which should be treated confidentially
		2.4	Describe the stages and components of the coaching process
		2.5	Describe how to plan coaching sessions that meet participant(s)' needs
		2.6	Explain how individual coaching sessions support the aims of the wider coaching programme
		2.7	Explain the process of setting SMART goals/objectives
		2.8	Describe how to start and end a coaching session
		2.9	Explain how the physical and psychological capabilities of participant(s) will influence the content and structure of the session
		2.10	Describe different types of demonstrations that encourage learning
		2.11	Explain how to balance instruction, facilitation, and demonstration within sessions
		2.12	Describe how to use listening skills
		2.13	Describe how to select language that is appropriate to participant(s)
		2.14	List how the coach can establish the views of participant(s) about the coaching sessions
		2.15	Identify situations when a coach may need to change or adapt a session
		2.16	Describe how to give constructive feedback to participant(s)
		2.17	Identify how to cater for an individual's needs within group coaching
		2.18	Describe how to organise group coaching sessions
3.	Understand participant(s)' learning styles	3.1	Outline different learning styles and needs
		3.2	Explain how to consider participant(s)' learning styles and needs when planning coaching sessions
		3.3	Describe the difference between the ways that adults and children learn
		3.4	Define the principles of monitoring and evaluating learning
		3.5	Describe how the coach can support participant(s) in taking responsibility for their own learning
		3.6	Describe how to manage different learning styles and learning needs, in group coaching

4.	Understand behaviour management	4.1	Identify the principles of positive behaviour management
		4.2	Describe how to develop a behaviour management strategy for coaching sessions
		4.3	Outline ground rules for positive behaviour during coaching sessions
		4.4	Outline the methods of communicating and implementing ground rules
		4.5	Explain the importance of fair and consistent behaviour management
		4.6	Explain how to encourage and reward positive behaviour
		4.7	identify the types of behaviour by participant(s) and others that may cause emotional distress
		4.8	Explain how to respond as a coach to behaviour by participant(s) that may cause emotional distress
		4.9	Describe how to respond to discriminatory behaviour
		4.10	Describe the procedures to be followed if a participant wants to complain about discrimination
5.	Understand how to reflect on a coaching session	5.1	Identify valid sources of feedback from participant(s) and support staff
		5.2	Explain how to do each of the following as part of self-reflection:
			• make self-assessment of skill level
			• identify action to be taken
			• use different methods of self-reflection
		5.3	Outline how to use evidence of own performance
		5.4	List factors that impact on the ability to identify own development needs
		5.5	Identify methods for personal action planning and the prioritisation of such planning
		5.6	Describe how to measure each of the following:
			• the quality of the coaching experience
			• participant development
			• the quality assurance mechanisms used
		5.7	Describe how to use information taken from evaluations to improve the programme/session

THEORY UNIT (TU) 2
Understanding how to develop participant(s) through coaching sport
2 credits/12 guided learning hours

Unit purpose and aims
This unit assesses the coach's understanding of the principles of planning, delivering and evaluating coaching sessions which improve participant(s)' performance in sport.

Learner Outcomes	Assessment Criteria	
The learner will:	The learner can:	
1. Understand the principles of planning coaching sessions	1.1	Identify the information required to plan coaching sessions
	1.2	Identify health and safety requirements that may impact on coaching sessions
	1.3	Describe how to establish goals for coaching sessions based on participant(s)' needs
	1.4	Identify sport-specific technical content to be included in coaching session plans
	1.5	List a range of coaching styles
	1.6	Explain the use of different coaching styles
	1.7	Describe how fun and enjoyment in coaching sessions can impact on learning
	1.8	Describe the components of planning a progressive coaching sessions
	1.9	Identify other appropriate people who can contribute to the delivery of coaching sessions and describe their potential contributions
	1.10	Describe how coaching sessions might be adapted as a result of Unforeseen changes to the coaching environment or participant(s)' needs
2. Understand the principles of skill development through coaching sessions	2.1	Define: • skill coordination • motor skill learning • skill acquisition • skill retention • skill transfer
	2.2	Describe the basic methods of analysing participant(s)' performance
	2.3	Identify factors that affect the development of participant(s)' skills in sport
	2.4	Describe the organisational requirements for the delivery of coaching sessions
	2.5	Describe the different techniques available for developing participant(s)' skill through coaching

		2.6	Identify methods to support participant development
		2.7	Identify sources of feedback which will support participant(s)' development
		2.8	Explain the importance of gaining feedback from participant(s)
3.	Understand the how the stages of participant(s)' development impact on their coaching	3.1	Describe the progressive stages of development through maturity
		3.2	Identify how the participant(s)' stage of development affects the content of coaching sessions
		3.3	Identify how participant(s)' stage of development impacts on the coaching environment
		3.4	Identify what influence training and competition have throughout the different stages of development
4.	Understand the principles of evaluation in coaching	4.1	Explain the principles of evaluating coaching sessions
		4.2	Identify a variety of evaluation methods that can be used to monitor participant(s)' development and learning
		4.3	Identify types of information that can be gathered to monitor participant(s)' development and learning
		4.4	Identify appropriate other people who can contribute to the evaluation of coaching sessions
		4.5	Describe how and when to gather information on current coaching practice from participant(s) and others
		4.6	Explain how the feedback from participant(s) and others should impact on future coaching practice
		4.7	Describe how to develop and record a personal action plan to improve own coaching practice, including highlighting opportunities for continuous professional development

THEORY UNIT (TU) 3
Supporting participant(s)' lifestyle through coaching sport
2 credits/16 guided learning hours

Unit purpose and aims

This unit assesses the coach's understanding of the lifestyle factors of nutrition, physical conditioning, mental preparation and awareness of drugs, which underpin performance in sport.

Learner Outcomes	Assessment Criteria
The learner will:	The learner can:
1. Understand basic nutrition and hydration principles for sports performance	1.1 Identify the five different food/nutritional groups
	1.2 Describe the principles of good nutrition as it relates to sports performance
	1.3 Describe the principles of hydration
	1.4 Identify the signs and symptoms of dehydration
	1.5 Describe the principles of weight management as appropriate to specific sports
	1.6 Explain how best to achieve optimum nutrition and hydration levels before, during and after training and competition
2. Understand physical conditioning for sport	2.1 Identify the components of physical and skill-related fitness
	2.2 Describe the physical capabilities required for a sport
	2.3 Describe the principles of injury prevention in training
	2.4 Describe how to support participant(s) in the management of injury
	2.5 Identify methods of training different physical components in participant(s)
	2.6 Identify the basic anatomy and biomechanical demands of a sport related activity
	2.7 Identify specific physical testing protocols for a sport related activity
	2.8 Identify methods to enhance participant recovery time from session to session
3. Understand principles of mental preparation in sport	3.1 Identify the mental capabilities required for a sport related activity
	3.2 Identify key methods for improving participant(s)': • confidence • concentration • motivation • emotional control • cohesion

		3.3	Describe the principles of participant(s)' development at the different stages of cognitive, emotional and social development
		3.4	Outline how a coach can profile participant(s)' mental skills
		3.5	Describe the basic coach intervention techniques for developing mental skills for training and competition
4.	Understand how to support participant awareness of drugs in sport	4.1	Outline the ethical issues surrounding drug taking in sport
		4.2	Identify sources of information on drugs in sport
		4.3	Outline the consequences for participant(s) in taking supplementation or prescription medicines

THEORY UNIT (TU) 4
Understanding the principles of safe and equitable coaching practice
2 credits/13 guided learning hours

Unit purpose and aims
This unit assesses the coach's understanding of how to ensure that their coaching is safe and equitable.

Learner Outcomes	Assessment Criteria
The learner will:	The learner can:
1. Understand how to ensure participant(s)' safety during sport-specific coaching sessions	1.1 Describe the health and safety requirements that are relevant to planned sport-specific activities and competition
	1.2 Describe how to structure coaching sessions to minimise the risk of injury to participant(s)
	1.3 Explain how to plan for contingencies to coaching sessions as a result of external influences
	1.4 Explain how to implement contingencies to coaching sessions as a result of external influences
	1.5 Describe the principles for checking the safe functionality of equipment used during sport-specific activities and competition
	1.6 Outline the main rules/regulations of the sport/activity appropriate to the level of the participant(s)
	1.7 Explain how to interpret and communicate the rules/regulations of the sport/activity to participant(s)
	1.8 Describe the coach's duty of care responsibilities for participant(s), including children
	1.9 Outline the coach's responsibilities for ensuring that the coaching environment is maintained appropriately
	1.10 Describe the following requirements for ensuring the protection of children from abuse: • legal requirements • sport-specific requirements
	1.11 Describe the insurance requirements on a coach operating in a coaching environment
2. Understand how to ensure equitable coaching of sport-specific activities	2.1 Describe the following requirements impacting on equitable coaching: • legal requirements • sport-specific requirements
	2.2 Explain the purpose of sport-specific Codes of Practice for coaching

	2.3	Explain how sport-specific Codes of Practice for coaching impact on coaching behaviour
	2.4	Describe methods to minimise barriers to participant development
	2.5	Explain what information is required in order to provide appropriate and safe opportunities for disabled participant(s) and specific populations
	2.6	Describe the nature of impairments and how their implications may affect aspects of the coaching process
	2.7	Describe how to identify coaching styles/delivery methods appropriate to variations in participant, task and environment
	2.8	Describe how and when to involve support staff to ensure participant(s)' needs are provided for within the coaching activity
	2.9	Describe how to adapt and progress activities and sessions
	2.10	Describe how to prepare athletes for competition
	2.11	Identify types of performance enhancing drugs and illegal substances
	2.12	Explain how a coach can discourage the use of performance enhancing drugs and any illegal substances

PTT
Theory Units

Theory Unit 1
Understanding the Fundamentals of Coaching Sport
3 Credits

Theory Unit 2
Understanding How to Develop Participant(s)
through Coaching Sport 2 Credits

Theory Unit 3
Supporting Participant(s)' Lifestyle through
Coaching Sport 2 Credits

Theory Unit 4
Understanding the Principles of Safe
and Equitable Coaching Practice 2 Credits

There are four theory units

Units 1, 2 and 4 are assessed in a group, and Unit 3 is assessed through the presentations. Candidates should prepare and bring the five presentations to the exam. They will be given one to deliver and the notes of the other four will be checked by the assessor.

The notes that follow in this book are designed to assist with practical answers for Units 1, 2 and 4. Although the learner outcomes and assessment criteria look complicated they will be assessed orally in a way that looks for practical answers.

The notes for Unit 3 (the presentations) are placed first. The notes for Units 1, 2 and 4 are not necessarily in chronological order relevant to the units, but they do give an outline of the information required for all three units.

General guidelines on presentations

People learn best when they are actively involved with the learning process. This helps their understanding and improves their interest and motivation to learn. It also allows them to build on their experience and relate information to prior knowledge and understanding.

With this in mind the classroom teaching section should reflect the above principles. Candidates are encouraged to move away from didactic (chalk and talk) approaches to this section. Instead the candidate should involve the group in an interactive, discussion style presentation. The use of visual aids should be used to facilitate this, through the use of a white/blackboard or flip chart.

Candidates are encouraged to use questions and answers to discover the group's prior subject knowledge. This information could be used to form the base for a discussion.

Lesson plans on each subject area should be prepared beforehand. These must be included in the portfolio. Lesson plans should be kept simple and allow the candidate to relate subject information to the groups prior knowledge of the subject area.

Each candidate is allocated up to ten minutes. It is important that candidates are realistic about how much content can be covered in this time and think carefully about time allocation when preparing their lesson plan. It is not necessary to use the whole 10 minutes to prove to assessors that candidates are up to standard in this section.

Below is an **example of a lesson plan**, which can be adapted for each subject area.

Subject: Nutritional advice for novice riders.

Resources required: White board and pens

Duration of lesson: Up to 10 minutes

Timing: Activity/content

0–2   Introduction to subject area and its importance.

2–4   Use questions to find out groups understanding of the benefits of healthy eating.

4–8   Discuss the 5 different food groups.

8–9   Ask group if they have any questions and give appropriate answers.

9–10   Conclude subject.

Self evaluation

_____

_____

_____

The following pages provide example content for various presentations. The information is not prescriptive nor comprehensive, and should not be copied 'word for word'. The bullet points suggest further key points that are suitable for inclusion. Candidates are encouraged to choose one of the key points for further discussion.

1. Nutritional advice for novice riders.

Horse riding can be a very demanding activity. Therefore it is important to eat a nutritious, balanced diet to provide sufficient fuel for your body. The base of the diet should come from carbohydrates in the form of starches and sugars to give energy. Protein,fats and vitamins and minerals are also required. This means eating a variety of foods every day such as grains, vegetables, fruits, beans, lean meat and low fat dairy products. Fluids, especially water, are very important.

Before exercise high carbohydrate foods, such as bananas, will be broken down quickly and provide glucose to the muscles. The timing of meals depends on the rider's preference for eating before exercise. Eating one to four hours before exercise helps keep plenty of blood glucose available for working muscles. Eating too close to exercise may cause stitch and can leave the rider feeling uncomfortable. It is important to drink plenty of water before exercise to keep muscles hydrated. The average person needs to drink six to eight glasses of fluid a day to prevent dehydration. Good hydration and a well-balanced diet are also thought to help reduce the likelihood of cramp. This can be common in the novice rider who will be more prone to fatigue and may lack general fitness.

It is suggested that any of the following subjects are suitable for inclusion within the discussion on nutritional advice:

- The healthy plate.

- The five different food types.

- Hydration.

- The signs and symptoms of dehydration.

- How best to achieve optimum nutrition and hydration before, during and after a session and competition.

- The principles of weight management for horse riders.

- The benefits of eating a balanced diet.

2. The importance of warm-up and cool-down for riders and horses.

It is essential to warm up horses and riders to ensure they are mentally and physically ready and to gain maximum benefit from a session.

Correct warming up techniques increase blood flow around the body, increasing the rider's and horse's flexibility and help to prevent injuries by increasing circulation and body temperature. Stretching will help prepare muscles for work and make them less prone to wear and tear. It is important to stretch each of the main muscle groups in the warm up.

Effective cooling down using light aerobic activity and gentle stretches will help to prevent muscle stiffness and aids recovery, ensuring that both horse and rider are mentally and physically ready to return to pre-training activities. It also helps the body dispose of waste products that have built up while exercising.

It is suggested that any of the following subjects are suitable for inclusion within the discussion on the importance of warm up and cool down advice:

- The reasons for warm up and cool clown.

- Injury prevention.

- Enhancing recovery time.

- Suitable exercises on the ground. Possibly get audience to participate. First check they do not have injuries.

- Suitable exercises mounted. Possibly get audience to participate. First check they do not have injuries.

- How warm up and warm down can speed up recovery time.

- The safety considerations of warming up enthusiastic horses.

- Safety considerations for warming up novice/beginner riders.

- How to recognise the horse and rider are warmed up enough.

- The use of stretching exercises.

- The importance of relating warm up to the work to be undertaken.

3. The physical requirements and conditioning for horse riding.

It is important that you are aware of what fitness components are required for riding and whether or not a rider is fit enough for the exercises to be undertaken in a session. Physical fitness includes aerobic endurance, muscular endurance, flexibility, speed, strength, power and body composition. Skill related fitness includes speed, agility, co-ordination, power, balance and reaction time. Riders also require suppleness, stamina and strength.

Many of the aspects of rider fitness can be enhanced by training off the horse. Weight training can improve muscle strength. Pilates and Yoga are popular ways of working on flexibility and core strength.

If rider fitness is not taken into consideration there is a much greater chance of injury. By ensuring that a rider is fit enough for the work to be undertaken and that the work is adapted for the individual rider then there is less possibility of injury. The work embarked on in the session should not cause undue pain or strain. If a rider is injured you may need to advise them to seek professional advice.

Riding places unique biomechanical demands on the rider, who needs to not only control their own body movements, but needs to absorb the horse's movement and react to his behaviour. This means that the stability of the rider's position is vital and needs good balance and co-ordination, straightness and symmetry. A good position reduces the possibility of injury. Knees, hips and ankle joints need to be flexible. Core stability is vital. As the coach you need to find out if the rider has any old injuries that may affect their position and that their body may compensate for.

If your rider agrees, it may be useful to test their readiness for riding. Sit ups are a good test of core strength. Press ups test endurance. Walking for the less fit and running for those who are fitter are a good indication of general fitness. Flexibility can be tested by a sit and reach test.

It is suggested that any of the following subjects are suitable for inclusion within the discussion on the physical requirements and conditioning advice:

- The componenets of physical fitness.

- The componenets of skill related related fitness.

- The physical requirements required for riding.

- Methods of training different physical components for riding.

- The basic anatomy and biomechanical demands of different riding activities.

- Testing available to assess fitness.

4. Mental preparation for riders.

The 4 Cs (concentration, confidence, control and commitment) are linked to successful riding.

Concentration is the rider's ability to maintain focus. This could be focusing on how they feel or on techniques appropriate to the task. Goal setting by breaking the goal into smaller sections such as a process or routine can be beneficial.

Confidence is vital for a rider to improve their skills. If a rider believes in their own ability their confidence will improve and they can start to take responsibility for their own learning. The coach can improve the rider's confidence by providing feedback and carefully preparing appropriate level activities and selected group work that builds on the rider's prior knowledge and skills. It is important to set goals that are shared, realistic and achievable.

Control is the ability to maintain self-control regardless of a distraction. This can be very challenging especially for children and young adults. The coach should provide support and encouragement, particularly in competitions when young riders may have difficulty in controlling negative emotion if they are not successful. The coach should focus on personal improvements in performance rather than rosettes (i.e. be process driven rather than outcome driven).

Commitment is the ability to continue working to agreed goals. The coach needs to understand the rider's motivation for completing the task and help by supporting the rider. The coach may need to adapt their coaching style in order to achieve this. Motivation can be improved by breaking goals into smaller ones and reminding the rider how smaller goals link to the overall aims of the programme and the agreed goal.

It is suggested that any of the following subjects are suitable for inclusion within the discussion on mental preparation for riding:

- The mental capabilities required for a riding related activity.

- Key methods for improving riders – confidence, concentration, emotional control, commitment (motivation).

- The principles of rider development in the different stages of cognitive, emotional and social development.

- How a coach can profile a rider's mental skills.

- The basic coach intervention techniques for developing mental skills for training and competition.

5. Drug awareness in riding.

It is important that a coach sets a positive example with regard to drug use in sport for both the horse and rider. The use of drugs leads to an unlevel playing field and a lack of fair play. Cheats can be ostracised from the sport and they may never regain any good name they had previously. This can impact on their long term reputation and ability to earn a living.

Information on drugs that may and may not be used for humans can be obtained from the WADA website (World Anti Doping Association). Information on drugs that may and may not be used for horses can be obtained from the FEI and BEF websites. Discussion with your local vet may also be useful.

If a rider is on medication of some sort they must obtain written proof from their doctor and ensure they have been cleared to use this medication by their Governing Body before competing.

The BEF have recently introduced changes to National Anti Doping and Controlled Medication rules which closely mirror those of the FEI for international competitions. The new system sees an increase in the number of anti-doping tests for affiliated competitions at all levels. All substances on the Prohibited List of drugs are known as Prohibited Substances. These are now divided into two groups – Banned Substances which should never be used and Controlled Medication Substances which are medication substances. It may be possible to obtain an Equine Therapeutic Use Exemption for a Controlled Medication Substance, but never for a Banned Substance.

Further details about anti-doping measures can be found on the BEF website.

It is suggested that any of the following subjects are suitable for inclusion within the discussion on understanding how to support participant awareness of drugs in sport:

- The ethical issues surrounding drug taking in sport.

- Where to find information about drugs in sport.

- What a competitor must do if taking supplements or prescription medicines.

What the assessor is looking for

- You must be able to give your presentation in a clear controlled voice, showing some variation in tone and volume as necessary.

- Your body language must show confidence and authority (avoid hands in pockets, looking down and talking into the floor).

- You should try to plan your subject so that you make a brief introduction, then content which includes clear facts, information and discussion, followed by a brief summing up and conclusion.

- You should prepare your presentation before your exam day. If you have had the opportunity to practise with an audience, this will help with your confidence.

- Try to ensure that you involve the audience as much as possible and avoid a pure 'chalk and talk' lecture.

How to become competent

- It is important that you feel comfortable when speaking to a small group of people with whom you are not familiar. You must achieve this by practising giving short prepared talks to your friends or co-students, so that you develop competence.

- Gradually try to get some practice in teaching groups of pony club or riding club members on familiar subjects.

- Practise preparing some of the suggested subjects for the presentation so that you have planned the introduction, the subject content, the summary and conclusion.

- Make sure that you practise the timing. There is not very long and it is important not to hurry to finish when the assessor asks you to bring the session to a close.

- When the assessor asks you to finish, or tells you that you have a minute or two remaining, make sure that you finish the sentence you are starting smoothly and with no change in the pace of your voice. Then state that you have no time left or have been asked to finish your presentation and ask if there are any questions, before thanking your audience and briefly summing up in your conclusion and asking one or two questions to test for learning.

- Your summing up should only be a sentence or two to conclude the talk; it should not end up being a brief run through of everything you have already said!

- You will probably give your presentation to the other members of your candidate group and the assessor(s) will sit at the back of the room or aside from the group you are addressing.

- Be confident enough to make eye contact with your audience; preferably stand to give your presentation as this carries more impact and authority than if you sit down.

- You may feel nervous and think your voice sounds shaky but to your audience this is rarely the case.

- If it helps to jot down a few bullet points on a postcard to act as prompters for you, this is fine, as long as you do not end up 'reading' your notes without lifting your head and looking at your audience.

- Avoid trying to say too much.

- Do give your presentation clearly and with a confident voice with variation in your voice tone.

- Do introduce the subject clearly.

- Do involve the audience.

- If you use a white board, write clearly, straight and with correct spelling. If you cannot do this then don't use a board.

- Practise giving these brief presentations frequently, if necessary to your friends and family, so that it is easy to do even when you are nervous.

PTT
Theory Units

Notes for Units 1, 2 and 4

Part A

What the assessor is looking for

- You should be able to discuss the procedure that your yard adopts for meeting and receiving strangers or visitors to the yard. All yards should have a procedure for receiving visitors. It is vital for security, and for visitors and clients to feel valued, that there is a procedure in place. Visitors should be welcomed with a smile and a 'Good morning/afternoon. Can I help you?' by all staff and students. In many yards staff and students are recognisable by either corporate clothing or a name badge. The office should be clearly marked and new visitors escorted there. Individual yards may have other procedures: for instance visitors are not allowed in close proximity to the horses unless accompanied by a member of staff. Be prepared to talk about any other procedures that are in place in yards that you know.

Enquiries by telephone should be answered politely, helpfully and efficiently. Potential customers should feel at ease and valued. There should be a general procedure for answering the phone. 'Good morning. Seaview Riding School. Mary speaking, how can I help you?' is much more user-friendly than a gruff 'Yes?'

Potential clients will want to know :

- what kind of riding school it is

- the qualifications of the staff

- the types of riding/activities available

- the types of horses/ponies available

- the times the school is open

- the costs

- where the school is

- they should also be informed that any new client is always given an assessment lesson before being put into a group or taken for a hack out

- You must be able to discuss information that would be essential to your riding school from a new client (e.g. height, weight, previous riding experience if any).

It is vital that you obtain certain basic information about all new riders. Existing rider documentation should be kept updated. You need to know their height, weight, age (if a child), previous riding experience and if they have any medical problems relevant to riding. You also need to know what their riding ambitions are. All this should be recorded on a rider registration form which must be signed by them.

- If a new client is starting to ride at your school you should be able to discuss with the assessor what information you would give to the client to help them feel at home when they come for their first riding lesson. You should also be able to discuss your assessment procedure for a new client, to enable you to fit the person into the most appropriate lesson situation.

All new clients should be assessed before they are allowed to join a class or go out on a hack. Some riding schools make the assessment the first lesson; others have a short assessment period before the lesson proper or the hack out. New clients should be informed when they book in that they will be assessed. Invariably, riders who are happy to do this will be at the level they say they are, and those who are not so happy are the ones who think they can ride but do not possess the appropriate level of skill.

There is a wealth of information that you could give to new riders, so you must be sure that they are not overloaded and therefore unable to remember everything. There is a first-class leaflet from the BHS entitled: 'Are you starting to ride?' which may be useful to have on hand to give to new riders.

It is vital to stress that jewellery should not be worn while riding. An easy way to convince people that they should not wear their largest gold-hooped earrings is to point out that not only are they a potential danger, but that they may also get lost in the school floor, never to be found again.

New riders cannot be expected to go out and purchase a set of riding gear – after

Rider Registration Form

The British Horse Society

Name of Equestrian Establishment: _____

Confidential - Please complete all sections below

First Name: _____ Surname: _____

Address: _____

_____ Postcode: _____

Tel: (home)_____ Tel: (mobile) _____

Email: _____

Date of Birth: _____ Age: _____ Weight: _____ Height: _____

Occupation: _____

Have you, or the rider you are signing for, ever suffered a serious injury or discomfort while riding or been advised not to ride? Yes ☐ No ☐

If yes, please describe: _____

Please detail any disability or medical conditions that may affect your ability to ride. This may include but not be limited to any back problems and any condition, which can affect balance or cause blackouts/loss of consciousness/fitting etc.

_____

_____

Emergency contact

Contact name and relationship: _____ Tel: _____

Riding ability/Declaration - you MUST tick all boxes that apply

| I consider myself (or the person riding for who I am signing on behalf as a minor) to be a: |
| Complete beginner ☐   Beginner ☐   Novice ☐   Intermediate ☐   Advanced ☐ |

| How many times have you/rider ridden in the past 12 months?   None ☐   Under 12 ☐   12-40 ☐   40+ ☐ |

| What do you believe your or the rider's capability to be on a horse or pony to be? |
| Riding at walk ☐   Trotting with stirrups ☐   Trotting without stirrups ☐   Cantering ☐   Hacking ☐ |
| Riding over jumps up to 0.5m (18") ☐   Riding over jumps 0.75m (30") ☐   Riding over cross-country jumps ☐ |

I confirm that to the best of my knowledge all of the above details are correct.
I have read the Horse Riders' Code of Conduct overleaf. I understand that riding at any standard has inherent risk that I may fall off and could be injured. I accept that risk and agree that the riding school will not be liable for injury or damage to property unless it is caused by their negligence.
Where I am signing on behalf of a minor I have explained the Riders' Code of Conduct to my child and we both accept the risk and agree that the riding school will not be liable for injury or damage to property unless it is caused by their negligence.
I have read and understand the lesson booking and cancellation policy and agree to bide by it at all times.
Data Protection Act 1998: Statement: I understand that the information I have given will be held in accordance with the Data Protection Act 1998 but may also be made available to Insurers and other concerned parties in the event of any injury or accident.

Signature: _____ Print Name: _____ Date: _____

If signed on behalf of a minor:

Rider's Name:_____ Relationship to minor:_____

To be completed by Instructor/Supervisor on behalf or the Equestrian Establishment

| This client has been assessed and our judgment of their capabilities is as follows: |
| Complete beginner (lead rein/lunge) ☐   Beginner (beginning walk and trot independently) ☐ |
| Novice (walk, trot, canter independently) ☐   Intermediate (jumping, Stage 1) ☐   Advanced (Stage 2, equivalent and above) ☐ |

Riders Name:_____

| **Assessment lesson content:** Walk ☐   Trot ☐   Canter ☐   W/O Stirrups ☐   Jump ☐   Lateral ☐ |

Horse used: _____ Lesson Type: _____

Date: _____ Time: _____

Signature: _____ Print Name: _____ Date:_____

all, they may have two or three lessons and then decide that riding is not for them.

Many riding schools hire out hats for new clients to wear and encourage riders to purchase their own hat as soon as they are sure they wish to continue with riding. Hats must be to current BSI standards and well maintained. If a school hat is dropped on the floor then it must be replaced, just as you would replace your own.

Riders should be encouraged to wear comfortable trousers – jeans are not really suitable as the seam on the inside of the leg is thick and can rub a rider's inner thighs. Jogging bottoms or leggings can be good if they are thick enough. Tight trousers are not suitable for obvious reasons. Clients must not be allowed to ride in shorts no matter how hot the weather.

Loose-fitting clothing that does not flap about is good for upper wear. Long sleeves are advisable, as they protect the skin of the arms in the event of a fall.

If riding outside, a waterproof coat is essential in wet weather.

Footwear is very important. Some riding schools hire out riding boots as well as hats. Stout lace-up shoes (for a child - school shoes) are acceptable. They must have a small, solid heel to stop the foot slipping through the stirrup. Buckles can catch on the stirrup; and fashion shoes are not strong enough. Trainers should not be allowed as there is no heel and they are not substantial enough. Wellingtons and boots with a thick-ridged sole are not good as the rider's foot can get stuck in the stirrup. Invariably with a beginner rider there has to be some give and take, but safety should never be compromised.

All riders should be encouraged to wear gloves as this will protect their hands from the reins and the cold in inclement weather conditions.

If not jumping, body protectors should be optional. Again, some riding schools hire them out; others insist that if riders wish to wear them they must purchase their own. It is advisable for riders who are going to jump to be encouraged to wear them. If going cross-country they should be mandatory as they are in competitions.

- You may be asked to discuss how you allocate horses to your pupils; this would include information about how you encourage riders to ride a range of horses in your school, including those they love and those that they are not so keen to ride. The allocation of horses and ponies to pupils is done in different ways, usually depending on the size of the establishment. It is vital that horses and ponies are not overworked and that their work load is varied so they do not become sour. A horse that is particularly good as a beginner's mount or is a really good lunge horse must be given the opportunity to hack out and be ridden by more experienced riders.

The number of hours a horse works per day depends on the type of work he is doing. A horse working at Stage 4 level may only be able to do two hours per day, but a horse undertaking less strenuous work may be able to do four hours a day as long as the work is spread throughout the day. All horses should have a day off a week. Some schools close for one day, others rotate horses' days off.

Beginners are best riding the same horse until they feel safe and confident. Riders tend to have their favourite mounts and sometimes it is difficult to convince them to change. If a hobby rider does not want to change then, although it would be better for their long-term progression to ride different horses, they should not be coerced into riding different horses. Riders who wish to progress, take exams or just continue to improve must ride a variety of horses to enhance their feel and technique. Often within a riding school there is one horse or pony that is not particularly popular, for whatever reason. Riders can be encouraged to ride this animal by employing a little psychology. By telling clients that you want them to ride this animal because they are going to help to improve it, or because you feel it will really help some particular part of their riding, or by using some other positive comments, you can often win them over.

If it is a real problem to convince clients to ride a particular horse or pony, then perhaps the school should consider selling him. It must be remembered that a client is a customer, and if customers do not like the experience they receive they are unlikely to return. (For example: there must be a shop or restaurant you will not go into because of the quality of service you have received).

When allocating horses it is important for the horses' sake that the tasks they undertake vary. Just because a horse is a good lunge horse does not mean he should do lunge lessons every day. He will soon become a poor lunge horse. Organising small shows on site, gymkhana games and obstacle courses can really help to help keep both clients and horses keen and interested. Many centres will not allow clients to take horses off site for competitions because of the risk of injury and/or the loss of revenue.

- You may have questions on methods of booking clients and taking payment for lessons. Each school will have its own method of recording bookings and payments. A booking-in sheet should be as simple as possible so there is no possibility of mistakes being made. Some schools use a book similar to those used in hairdressers', with the instructors' names at the top of each column. Others use a simple diary. At some schools only certain members of staff are allowed to book in clients; at others any member of staff who is trained may book in clients. It is important that no mistakes are made. A client who arrives for a lesson at a given time will not be very happy if they find there have been changes made. There should be a cancellation policy for both the school and clients. Both parties should strictly adhere to this. Many riding schools have a policy of insisting that any lesson not cancelled 24 hours in advance must be paid for.

Payments are usually made before the lesson. Monies received should be recorded. Some schools have a till with a receipts payment roll, which also means that the client receives a receipt. Other schools simply write the payment in a column in the booking-in register and this is added up at the end of each day and checked against the monies taken. Money should be securely stored and banked regularly.

- You may be asked about client retention schemes and you should have ideas on these. You should be able to talk about 'pony for the day' days, incentive schemes to encourage riders to book several lessons in advance or reduction schemes on courses or lessons booked in 'bulk'.

There are many ways in which riding schools can try to retain their clients. Probably the best way is to ensure that staff are friendly, interested in the clients, the school is well organised, and the horses are of a good standard and are right for the jobs they have to undertake. Other ideas such as working towards qualifications whether they are the BHS Stages, Progressive Riding Tests, Riding and Road Safety Test or the Horse Owners' Certificates can keep clients engaged. Holding small internal competitions can provide a real focus for those who have a competitive streak. An 'own a pony/horse' day or week can be demanding to organise and run and requires adequate staff and facilities for success, but such days are usually well attended and can be lucrative. Hacks out can keep riders and horses positive. Some riding schools have incentive schemes for clients to purchase lessons in advance in bulk – for example, they may purchase six lessons and get one free. This has the advantage of money being available in advance and there is less administration to do at the beginning of each lesson.

- You should be able to discuss procedures for assessing clients prior to taking them for a hack.

  If any riders are assessed as not competent enough to hack out, they should be offered a lesson instead. On arrival, they should fill out the usual rider registration form and, if wishing to hack out, they should be assessed in the paces they will be riding on the hack. It is also important to assess their confidence, as this can affect the decision as to whether or not it is safe to take them out.

- Have some ideas about how many riders should be taken in one riding lesson. This may vary according to the level of competence of the riders, the ability of the instructor, the nature of the work they hope to do (e.g. an advanced lesson taken by an experienced instructor might have six to eight riders, whereas a less experienced instructor may only be able to cope with three or four riders).

- It is important that the riding surface be kept in good condition. If a track appears around the outside of the school this should be filled in daily to ensure the horses' fetlocks are not constantly being twisted. Different surfaces need different maintenance. All surfaces must be kept flat. If they need watering to stop dust this must be undertaken as often as is necessary. This may be twice a day in hot weather. Dusty surfaces are bad for horses', riders' and coaches' lungs. Some surfaces need harrowing regularly to prevent them becoming 'dead' to ride on. Others need the droppings picked up to maintain the quality of the surface.

- Kickboards should be kept clean, as should mirrors and the gallery (if one exists). If there are notice boards these should be kept up to date and tidy. Nothing looks worse than a notice board with dog-eared pieces of dirty paper pinned to it in a haphazard manner.

- Equipment used regularly on a surface must be kept tidy and safe. Jump wings and poles can be expensive and if they are well maintained they will last longer. They should be regularly painted. Poles can be stored on the walls of an indoor school or on a rack outside an outdoor surface. Wings should only stay in the school if they are going to be used that day. 'Bloks' are really versatile as they can be used for jumps and obstacle courses. Anything made of plastic will eventually crack if left out in the elements for too long. Equipment that is well maintained and stored tidily helps to give the impression of a well-run establishment where people care.

How to become competent

- It is essential that you gain some experience in a commercial riding school, even if you are only able to assist at the weekend, it is still the most valuable way of seeing the clientele of a centre and dealing with the day-to-day issues.

- Find out where the school sources its new clients. Does it regularly advertise in the local press or do riders come through recommendation and word of mouth?

- Are new clients encouraged to come and visit the centre and speak face-to-face with a member of staff? They should be shown around the yard so that they feel familiar with where they will come for their first lesson. They should be shown where the office is, where the loo or rest room is, where the indoor or outdoor arena is and where the horses are.

- There should be a system in place which enables clients to see which horse they have been allocated. In their early lessons, a client should have a member of staff available to help find the horse and bring it out to the school and mount. Many schools have a daily sheet which is displayed on a prominent noticeboard for all to see. Ask if you can become involved in the preparation of this daily sheet so you are able to learn what is required. New clients should have a member of staff available to help them understand the sheet and to get their horse for them and help them mount until they are confident with the processes and regulation involved.

- Be aware that a new rider should be advised on what is safe and appropriate clothing for riding. Do not assume that they will know that a correctly fitting riding hat of a current BSI safety standard is essential. Make sure that you know whether your school hires hats to the clients or not, or whether they may borrow one for the first few lessons before being advised to invest in their own.

- Be able to advise on safe footwear, either riding boots, paddock boots or sturdy walking type shoes with a small heel, preferably laced and without a heavy ridged sole. Wellington boots and trainers are not safe, as they may get stuck in a stirrup or slip through respectively.

- Learn to accumulate information systematically from any or all of your clients to include, name, address, contact telephone numbers, age, a person to contact (especially with children) in an emergency. Approximate height, weight, previous experience if any. Any disabilities or medical issues, e.g. asthma, diabetes.

- Information that the client should receive from you (the centre) would include advice on clothing as listed, procedure on arrival at the school (e.g. book in the office and pay in advance).

- Your aim should be to make your clients feel supported and comfortable about coming to the school, but nevertheless clear about the rules in the centre (e.g. no feeding tit-bits to any horses, only bring horses to the school when instructed to do so by your instructor).

- Get to know the booking process of your centre. If you can, become involved in this so you can see how double booking is avoided and non-peak times are filled. Check the cancellation policy of your centre. Some centres do not enforce this policy strictly – if so, find out why this is the case.

- Find out what the payment policy is at your centre and why that policy has been adopted. Whatever it is, it must be clear, understandable and accountable.

- Discuss with your centre any incentive schemes they have for clients. Try to become involved in assessments that are taking place as well as assisting with lessons and hacks. The more practical hands-on experience you get the more practical your answers will be. You will then show the assessor that you are experienced and understand what is involved.

- Discuss with your instructor what his/her feelings are about class numbers. If you are at a riding school then discuss with the proprietor or chief instructor the reasons for the lesson sizes they adopt. The decision has to be a balancing act between commercial viability, health and safety issues and the experience of coach and riders.

- Volunteer to act as a second escort on hacks. This will help you to understand the potential problems and how they can be prevented. It will also help you to understand the matter of horse allocation and customer service. There is a fine line between keeping some customers satisfied and ensuring that health and safety issues are kept as a priority.

Part B

What the assessor is looking for

- You may be asked about grading riders at different levels of ability. Consider the advantages (e.g. everyone working at the same standard, work chosen by the teacher can suit everyone) and also consider some of the disadvantages (e.g. no one of a higher standard within the ride to demonstrate a new exercise or piece of work for the other riders). Sometimes, in spite of all being the same standard some riders may be more ambitious and hard-working than others.

  It is very useful to grade clients into riders that are of similar ability. It is easier for the coach to help the group as they can all work on similar issues. The horses will also all tend to be of a similar standard and this will mean that no horse or rider will be overfaced.

  If you have a ride of mixed ability riders, the better riders may become bored and the less experienced riders may feel, at best, incompetent, and, at worst, overfaced, worried and demoralised. It is important that the exercises the ride is asked to undertake are geared at the level of the rider of the lowest ability. Consequently you can see how easy it would be for a very experienced rider to become dissatisfied with their lesson. It is useful, however, sometimes to have a more experienced rider in a lesson if you wish to have particular exercises demonstrated. A better rider can also act as a role model for other riders to aspire to.

  Riders of a similar standard can encourage each other in their lessons and out of lesson time. They can share their issues and then realise that they are not the only ones who find certain activities difficult.

  Some riders will progress more quickly than others, and as riders improve their goals may change. In these circumstances riders may wish to change groups and this should be discussed with those responsible for group organisation.

It is important to assess new riders before putting them into a group. Many riders overestimate their own capabilities. New riders coming into an established group can help to refresh the ride, but if they are not of a suitable standard then this can lead to the existing riders becoming disgruntled. It must always be remembered that as riding instructors, teachers/coaches we are offering a service to the public and as such they must be treated as valued customers. If they become unhappy they will leave and take their custom to another riding school.

- You may be asked about leaders for beginner riders in a class lead-rein lesson. You should be able to talk about the age and competence of these helpers and that they would be the responsibility of whoever was teaching the lesson.

If you have a group of leaders for a beginners' ride it is important that they understand what they should do. They are there to ensure the riders' safety and control the ponies when necessary. They are not there to teach the riders. It is confusing for the riders if two people are telling them what to do. The helpers should be told that they must only pass on an instruction that you, as the coach, ask them to. You may, for example, ask them to help a beginner to hold the reins correctly, but they should only undertake this when you request it.

When they are leading a pony they must ensure that they have control and that they are concentrating on what is happening. It is a very responsible role to be the leader of a beginner rider and leaders should be encouraged, thanked and praised. You may suggest to them that perhaps they would like to work towards their UKCC Level 1 qualification. Candidates can register for this qualification at the age of 14, although they cannot take the final assessment until the age of 16. They might also like to work towards the Riding Schools Assistant Certificate of Competence which they can take at the age of thirteen.

- You will be asked in some detail about different types of lesson. Have some ideas about the value of individual lessons as compared with class lessons; there are always disadvantages as well as advantages (e.g. the advantage of one-to-one individual help needs to be weighed against the possible demoralising effects on pupils who have no one to compare themselves with).

There are several different types of lesson that a customer can choose from. A private lesson ensures that a rider has one-to-one attention and tuition from the coach. Private lessons are very good for novice riders until they are at a standard where they can control a horse competently and are confident enough to join a group. Private lessons are also useful for riders who wish to take their riding very seriously and possibly go on to compete. Private lessons can also build up a rider's confidence quickly as the exercises used will be specific to the individual. They are, of course, more expensive, which can be an issue for some riders. They are also more intensive, so may be of a shorter duration – maybe three quarters of an hour rather than an hour.

- Be clear on the value of a – possibly costly – individual lesson (e.g. for a serious competition rider) versus a group lesson, where there can be camaraderie, motivation to be as good as your friend and a fun social experience.

A class lesson is more social for the riders and can be less intense. The riders have an opportunity to build up a relationship with each other, and can learn by watching each other. The coach needs to be very well organised and ensure that everybody is catered for. All the riders need to feel that they have achieved something during the lesson and that it has been worthwhile for them. Healthy competition between riders can help with progress, but riders can, however, become demoralised if they observe others who constantly seem to be better than they are. Class lessons can easily be made fun for riders who ride for leisure. A class lesson is more viable for a centre, but it is important that the maximum number of riders is restricted so that each rider is happy with the attention they receive.

- Understand the value of beginners starting to learn to ride on a lead rein (or perhaps even the first time on a mechanical horse) or on the lunge.

Lunge lessons are very good for helping the rider to improve their position. Because the coach is responsible for the way the horse goes, the rider can concentrate on his or her own body. A complete beginner may not always benefit from a lunge lesson – if they are nervous or worried they may find it difficult to relax when the person in control of the horse is at the other end of a long rein holding a big whip! A lunge lesson can be intense for both horse and rider, and the coach must ensure that they do not overwork either of them. A novice rider can make huge strides in their position with a few lunge lessons, and the more serious rider can keep their position polished and workmanlike by being lunged.

Lunge lessons are usually only half an hour's duration because of the intensity of the work.

For a beginner adult or child lead-rein lessons are a very useful way of starting. An adult may only need one or two lead-rein lessons to get them started, but the confidence gained from having somebody nearby and helping to control the horse can be very important. For adults, a lead-rein lesson may be better as a private lesson as older people can be embarrassed about their lack of ability to undertake new tasks. Many riding schools have class lead-rein lessons for beginner children. As long as there are enough leaders then this is a viable and fun way of introducing children to riding. Without the leaders it is very difficult to have the control necessary, and a beginner class lesson with children who are not being led, can be chaotic.

It is useful to have stable management sessions available for customers to learn how to look after horses and ponies correctly. Many riders will eventually want to own their own horse and will appreciate having the opportunity to learn the skills required. Riders can be encouraged to take the Progressive Riding Tests and the Horse Owners' Certificates. This can also be a useful income stream on days when the weather is too bad to ride or there are other circumstances where horses are unavailable. If customers learn the skills correctly it will also be beneficial for the welfare of the horses at the school as they will be more correct and consistent in their handling.

Hacking out is something that many riders aspire to and can also be beneficial for the horses. The majority of riders have no desire to become top competition riders and use their riding as a form of stress buster. What better way to relax than to take a hack out in the fresh air on a well-behaved horse.

- Be clear about your responsibility if you were escorting a hack on the roads, open spaces or bridleways. It is important, through the initial assessment and subsequent booking of a hack, that the pupils know exactly how competent they should be (e.g. able to walk, trot and canter independently) before hacking, and that they must take some responsibility for their own control and safety on the ride.

The organisation of a hack must be carefully considered and horses and riders must be carefully matched. The person in charge of the hack must be very experienced and it is advisable for them to hold at least the BET Assistant Rider

Leader qualification. If riders were hacking often on the road then the Riding and Road Safety Test would be an advisable option to train for and achieve.

If the riders are not known to the riding school they must be assessed in all the paces that will be used on the hack before being allowed out. The usual rider registration forms must have been filled out. With a group hack it is always best to have a rear escort as well as a leader, who should be the person with overall responsibility. The leader is responsible for the safety of the riders and horses and the paces and the terrain covered must be suitable for the person of the lowest ability to cope with.

Before leaving for the hack, riders' attire and stirrup lengths must be checked, along with the rest of the horses' tack and tightness of their girths. The riders should be informed of the rules they have to abide by. The most important rule is that they must do as they are told by the leader. The second most important rule is that they must not overtake the rider in front of them. To ensure this is successful the horses must be placed in order with the most forward-thinking ones at the front. The leader must tell those who are left at the school where they are going and how long they will be out. They should take a pack out with them that includes a mobile phone or money for a phone box and a simple first-aid kit and a hoof pick. It is also useful to take a lead rein in case it becomes necessary to lead one of the horses. The leader and rear escort must know the riders' names so they can communicate with them quickly to give advice, build rapport and give commands.

The leader must set the pace and always let the ride know when they are going to undertake a transition and ensure these are done safely. If a leader suddenly stops it can cause the rest of the ride to 'crash' into them and create a 'domino effect'. If the ride is going to canter then the location must be carefully selected. The best place is a slight uphill path that is fairly enclosed on both sides so that overtaking is not possible. Such an ideal place may not be available, but it may be possible to canter parallel to a hedge, which would help with control. It is better not to canter on the way home.

Hacking out can be difficult when there are only a limited number of rides and canter places. Horses, being creatures of habit, can start to anticipate a canter, become excited and start to misbehave. Riders usually like to have a canter and feel cheated if they don't. It may be useful to take staff out on the hacks and not to canter in the usual places to help break the routine of always doing the same thing in the same place.

The leader and back-up rider should stay alert at all times, observing the riders and looking out for hazards.

It is important when riding on the roads to have knowledge of the Highway Code and to follow its rules. When riding in the countryside always follow the Country Code. The most important points are: always leave gates as you found them; keep to designated paths; ride round the boundary of a field and do not disturb livestock; walk when riding near pedestrians; and do not overtake other riders without their permission.

- You may be asked about factors in a lesson that might contribute to the horse or rider feeling uncomfortable or anxious. Consider the intensity of the lesson with riders who may only ride once a week. Physically they may not be very fit if they do not take any other exercise at all. Even walking the dog, walking to the bus or a weekly swim helps the rider's overall fitness. Hot weather may cause the horses to sweat excessively and therefore become distressed if work is over demanding. The horse may already have done two hours' work during the day and the lesson content should take into consideration the horse and rider's ability to fulfil the work chosen.

- The assessor will expect you to recognise when a child or adult rider is not coping physically or mentally with the work of the lesson.

It is important that, as a coach, you are aware of how your riders are feeling. If they become distressed or are in discomfort they may not tell you. They just will not turn up for their next lesson. Many riders will not tell you if they are in pain or are finding exercises really difficult. Always remember that many riders will not be as fit as you are. A rider's physical shape must be taken into account and this needs to be considered when allocating their mount. For instance, a person who has a short leg length may find a wide cob uncomfortable to ride.

It is easy to ask too much from a beginner or novice rider. Asking for sitting trot for too long, working for extended periods without stirrups, or pushing too hard when trying to teach the rising trot can all lead to a rider becoming physically exhausted. Once the body becomes tired a rider will not be able to control what they are doing so well and progress will be slow. Signs that a rider is becoming physically and/or mentally tired include not being able to maintain the body in the required position, red or very pale face, lack of concentration, shortness of breath, not being able to remain still, facial expression, crying and shortness of temper.

Riders who are worried about something may well talk a lot or may be quieter than usual. They may also stress the fact that they can't do this or that, focussing on their inadequacies rather than their abilities. A rider who is nervous may flatly refuse to ride a particular horse or ask not to try exercises that are out of their comfort zone. Such a request must be respected. If a rider is not happy to try an exercise then the chances they will not be successful are high.

Very hot and very cold weather can create issues. If the weather is very hot the rider may start to become dehydrated and lose concentration and body strength. Very cold weather can lead to the rider becoming stiff and losing feeling in their fingers and toes. Nobody can concentrate in these circumstances! It is vital that you stay alert to signs of distress. In a private lesson a rider may discuss this with you, but in a class lesson they may be too embarrassed to talk about it. Some children will go away from a lesson in real pain and not tell you, whereas others will let you know as soon as there is a trivial issue. It all comes down to observing and getting to know your clients. Building up a good relationship and rapport is essential. Always treat your riders as you would like to be treated yourself.

Weekly riders may well arrive for their lesson thinking about issues that have nothing to do with riding. An adult may have had a particularly difficult day at work, or a child might have had a mishap in the playground that day. These issues can mean that they will be unable to concentrate fully on their riding and are tense and unsettled. This may lead to exercises not being carried out correctly, which in turn may lead to frustration and further tension.

Some mature beginners may not be able to achieve the 'classical' position. As coaches it is important for us to realise that stiffness may be a real issue and that the 'ear–shoulder–hip–heel' line may be totally unachievable. As a coach you must be prepared to compromise and try to ensure that the rider works towards achieving the best position they can, working towards achieving harmony with the horse they are riding. There is a world of difference between teaching a leisure rider and somebody who wants to become a professional in the equine industry and/or a competitor.

- You should be able to describe the general format of any lesson. Be clear that any lesson of any duration must have an introduction and a period of warming up both horse and rider; during this time an assessment can be made of both the rider's ability and how appropriate the horse is for the rider. The main content of the lesson will be chosen on the findings of the assessment and the latter part of the lesson should include a clear summary of the work and a conclusion so that the rider(s) go away with confidence and understanding of what to aim for or be able to work for the next time.

The general format of a lesson is the same for whatever the length of session. All lessons should be pre-planned and have a structure so that there is a logical sequence and the riders feel they are progressing.

There are four main phases of a lesson:

The Introduction During the introduction the coach should introduce himself or herself and, if they do not know the riders and the horses, should find out some information about each rider and horse. There should be a brief tack check, including the girths and equality of stirrup length, and the riders' clothing should be observed. The aims of the lesson should be discussed and, depending on the level of the lesson, there could be some discussion with the riders as to which exercises they could use. There could also be a discussion as to whether or not the riders have undertaken any loosening exercises before mounting.

The ride should then be warmed up. This is an important time for horse, rider and coach. This period should consist of simple exercises to supple muscles and tendons in both the horses and riders, and the coach can also use it as a time of assessment. Girths can be re checked and stirrups altered if necessary.

The main lesson content During this phase the main aim of the lesson is worked towards and hopefully achieved. Whatever the lesson content, it must always be relevant to the levels and capabilities of the riders and coach. The work should progress logically and the ride must be given short rest periods so they do not become fatigued. Rest periods must be used tactfully as riders may feel they have spent a lot of time standing still and doing nothing. If a new topic is to be taught then do remember the different ways in which people learn (see pages 97 to 103). Any new topic should be explained and demonstrated and then the riders should be given ample opportunity to practise, practise, practise. It is only by repetition that a new skill can be learnt and assimilated.

As a coach you may well need to have several different ways of putting the same point over, and have patience to help riders improve. To ask a pupil to repeat the same thing in the same way, over and over again, can become de-motivating for that rider. Take every opportunity to observe high-quality coaches and assimilate good ideas into your own repertoire of teaching skills.

The conclusion During this phase the riders and horses should be given the opportunity to 'cool down' by undertaking some stretching work. There should be discussion of what has been learned, and the coach should check the riders' knowledge and understanding by asking questions. The riders should be given an opportunity to ask questions. Each rider should be given feedback as to how they have done and a brief action plan as to how they can move forward during the next session. If the coach has assessed the situation as safe, all this could be done at walk on a long rein, which would aid the cool-down process.

Self-reflection The final part of the lesson is where the coach takes the opportunity to self-reflect on how the session has gone. This is absolutely vital if we are to improve our techniques and become better coaches. Always look for the positives first and remember to take these forward for a similar lesson in the future. Then look for the things that did not go as well as you thought and try and work out why this was. Was it because the exercise was too hard for the riders/horses? Were the riders distracted by something? Were the horse and rider combinations unsuitable? Were you explanations muddled? The list is endless. Only by deciding where things went wrong (if they did) can we work to ensure the same issues do not happen again.

• When making a long term plan for a rider it is important to ensure that you do not assume any prior knowledge. When a beginner comes for their first lesson they may well not know what a girth or the pommel are. There is a huge equine language which those in the industry use daily, but which newcomers have to learn. If we are not careful, a beginner can quickly start to feel inadequate before they have even mounted the horse.

There is no one sequence in which riders should be taught, but there are basic principles that must apply. The most important factor to be taken into consideration is the safety of the rider and horse.

A beginner may well start with lead-rein lessons. They will initially be taught how to check their stirrup length and girth and then how to mount. It is easier for a beginner to learn to mount from a mounting block. This is also better for the horse's back and for the saddle. There is a real skill in giving and receiving a leg-up and a beginner will not have the ability to take a leg-up well. Mounting from the ground can be difficult for a beginner as they may not have the 'spring' required to do this. The coach must always check the girth and tack and assist the rider in any way necessary. Some riding schools give beginners the reins straight away, while others make the rider hold the saddle or neck strap until they are a little more confident.

Once the rider is confident in walk they can be taught a little sitting trot. Some riders find it interesting to be taught the sequence of legs as they learn to undertake walk and trot, but others find this is information overload. Once they can feel the rhythm of the sitting trot, the rising trot can be taught. It is easier for horse and rider if they practise the rising technique at the halt and then at the walk before trying it in the trot. The rider should be encouraged to move the hips forward a little as they rise, and not allow the feet to push the stirrups forward. When the rising trot is established and the rider can rise independently of the hands, diagonals can be taught. Some people teach canter before diagonals and others teach trotting poles before canter. As long as there is a methodology that works for you and your horses, that is acceptable.

When teaching diagonals it is easier for a rider to see how the horse's legs move if the diagonal pairs of legs are fitted with different coloured boots or bandages. Although we should work towards the rider feeling the diagonal, it is usually easier initially to teach them to watch the outside shoulder until they have mastered the technique. Once this is established they can move on to starting to feel the movement.

Right from the beginning it is important to involve the rider in their learning and to ask them for feedback on how they are coping and what they can feel from the movement of the horse.

As soon as a rider is confident riding with their stirrups they should be introduced to work without stirrups. This can be in walk initially and built up to trot as confidence increases. Riding without stirrups is so beneficial for balance and position it is something that every rider should be encouraged to try.

Teaching a person to canter is one of the most difficult things to do in riding.

Riding schools will have their own methods for doing this, but it is important that nobody is forced into trying to canter if they do not want to, and that the horses used are the right ones for the job and are schooled for the task. As a coach you cannot expect a rider to remember the complicated aids for canter when they are excited and/or apprehensive about what is going to happen. A rider will need to be told how to apply a basic aid to canter (hold the neck strap/pommel with one hand, sit up and use the legs) and the coach may well have to use their voice to help the horse into the pace. The coach can explain to the rider that as they become proficient more subtle aids to ask a horse to canter can be applied. A few strides of canter is enough for the first attempt. If the horse canters for too long the rider may well tip forward and lose balance.

School figures: Riders should be encouraged to ride school figures accurately and smoothly, and once they are proficient they should understand how their position and aids can affect the way in which the horse performs these. By learning to ride accurate school figures the rider learns how to prepare a horse for a movement, and self-discipline, which is vital for anyone wishing to become a genuinely educated rider.

Circles are usually of 20m, 15m or 10m diameter. Page 26 shows the most usual places to ride them in a 20 x 40m arena.

As riders become more efficient they can be introduced to more difficult figures.

Half circles (see page 26) of various sizes can be used to change the rein.

A 5m loop (see page 26) appears easy, but to ride one accurately and keep the horse in balance while doing so, is a real skill.

A three-loop serpentine (shown on page 26) needs thought and preparation to ensure the horse maintains balance and that the figure is symmetrical.

Once the rider is proficient in canter they may well want to start to hack out. If they have done some work over poles and in the light seat then they can apply this technique while out hacking if the necessity arises.

When introducing jumping it is very important again that the rider wants to learn to jump and that the horse is the right one for the job. More people stop jumping because they have learnt on unsuitable horses and have 'lost their nerve' than carry on and enjoy the skill. If the rider has not already learned the light seat with shortened stirrups then this must be taught first. The rider must learn to be secure through the lower leg in the light seat before they attempt a jump. They should also be happy in the light seat over trotting poles.

A first jump should be a single cross-pole, and the rider must hold a high neck strap whilst attempting this. This is for the sake of the horse as much as for the rider. Once the rider is happy going over a single fence in trot they can move on to a second fence. This fence should not be at a related distance to the first fence. If the first fence is at B (off the track) then the second fence could be off the track at E. This gives the rider plenty of time to rebalance him/herself before attempting a second fence. A third fence can be put across the diagonal, which starts to introduce the idea of a small course. Once the rider is confident putting a small number of fences together they can then be introduced to grid work.

As confidence improves, the height of the fences can be raised a hole at a time until the rider is happy jumping at Stage 2 height. It must be remembered that to pass Stage 2 jumping, the candidate must be confident enough to get on two unfamiliar horses and jump them round a course. This means that they must practise jumping as many different types of horse as possible. A rider who is only happy to jump the same horse will not be successful in Stage 2 jumping.

- Linked into the progression described above, you may well be asked to give examples of when riders should hold the saddle, neck strap and reins.

It is very important that a beginner and novice rider have a neck strap of some kind to use when necessary. As already mentioned some riding schools do not allow beginners to hold the reins until they are capable in rising trot. Other schools allow beginners to hold the reins from the first lesson, but make the riders hold the neck strap with one or both hands for trot work. Sometimes the reins are tied in a knot, and sometimes the rider puts the reins into one hand and holds the neck strap with the other; at other times the reins are slipped through the fingers and the pommel is held at the same time. This can be a huge handful for a child with small hands, so care must be taken.

Riders should be encouraged to hold the front of the saddle or the neck strap whenever they feel unsafe; by doing so they do not interfere with the horse's mouth. If the rider is already behind the movement with their weight distribution then holding the pommel can encourage the weight to go further back, whereas holding the neck strap can encourage the rider to come a little more forward.

When deciding whether or not to hold the neck strap, pommel and/or reins the security of the rider and the welfare of the horse are the two main priorities that need to be considered.

- You may be asked to discuss activities that are aimed at giving children fun in lessons.

There are a huge range of activities that can make learning fun for children. Some examples are:

Gymkhana games – mounted and dismounted

Obstacle courses/handy pony

Inter-group competitions

Fancy dress (especially at Christmas/Easter)

Speed exercises – e.g. fastest round the world

Drill/musical rides

Riding to music

'Follow the leader'

'Simon says'/imitating the coach

Learning names of colours/tack/points of the pony, etc.

Touching the school letters and thinking of a word beginning with that letter

Riding round, through, and over poles set in various patterns

Working towards the Progressive Riding Tests

- You should be able to explain how you would teach new exercises.

When a new task is learnt it is important for coaches to understand how it is learnt so that they can help their pupils at each stage and recognise the issues that are there to do this.

Before a rider starts to jump they must be secure in the light seat. It is possible for riders to become confused when talking about light seat/jumping position. It is important that you describe clearly what you mean to your riders so they understand and are on the same wavelength as you. Light seat generally tends to be described as a position of the upper body between the normal flatwork position and the fold adopted over a jump. It can also be called the poised position, the forward seat or half seat. Some people also call this the jumping position and do not distinguish between this 'half-way' position and the fold over a fence. As you can see with all these different definitions and terms it is important that you and the riders understand each other. It is also important that you, your riders and the assessor are talking about the same thing.

There is much discussion about how many poles you should put out after one. It is generally accepted that if the poles are placed 9 ft/2.7 metres apart then you can go from one to two poles. If the poles are placed closer so the horse has to step over a pole every step then it is safer to go from one to three poles. The horse should then not think he has to jump them. The accepted distance for trotting poles for an 'average' horse is 4ft 6ins/1.4m. For a pony it can be as small as 3ft 6ins/1.06m.

You must learn :

(a) how to walk pole and jump distances accurately so you know how large your stride is;

(b) pole and jump distances;

(c) to tell when the distances you have set for horse/ponies is not comfortable for them and be able to alter them so they are safe.

Distances for an 'average' horse of about 15.2hh:

Trotting poles: 4ft 6ins/1.4m

One non-jumping stride between two fences (trot approach): 18ft/5.4m

One non-jumping stride between two fences(canter approach): 21ft/6.4m

One non-jumping stride between two fences (competition distance): 24ft/7.3m

Two non-jumping strides between fences (trot approach): 30ft/9.1m

Two non-jumping strides between fences (canter approach): 33ft/10m

A related distance of three strides with a canter approach: 45ft/13.7m

Bounce fence – no strides between two fences (not to be used with novice riders): 10–12ft/3–3.6m

Placing pole in front of a fence (trot approach) 8–9ft/2.4–2.7m

When placing a pole in front of a fence to be approached in canter, unless you are using the pole to help with a specific problem, it is better to put the pole one or two canter strides away. A placing pole can be very useful for setting up a horse and rider to reach the correct take-off point for the jump, but can also discourage some horses from thinking forward to a fence.

It must be remembered that the above distances are only a guide to work from and the coach must learn to assess how a horse is working through poles and jumps and alter them accordingly.

There are five phases to the jump:

the approach to the fence

the take-off

the flight

the landing

the getaway (which can be the approach to the next fence)

The phases of jumping

The rider should understand that a good approach is vital, with rhythm and balance being maintained and with the horse being presented straight at the middle of the fence. The rider cannot, however, be expected to worry about this until they are happy going over a fence. The same applies to the getaway.

- You will be asked about the benefits of using ground poles, placing poles, grids and related distances. You must also be able to discuss basic grid construction and how to estimate the distances between one jump and another.

Gridwork is excellent for both horses and riders. It improves the rider's position and can help to increase their concentration. It helps increase suppleness and athleticism in both horses and riders and can help to build up their muscle tone. If the grid is set at comfortable distances for the horse it can help enhance their balance, rhythm, co-ordination and bascule. By changing the distances within a grid a horse can be helped to lengthen or shorten his stride and bascule. This type of gridwork should only be undertaken with very competent and confident riders who can help the horse in his way of going if necessary, and be able to ride through the grid without detriment to his action.

Gridwork should not be attempted with novice jump riders. Although it may appear easy because the jumps are set so that the horse goes through the grid and the rider just has to follow, if the rider is not secure and well balanced when jumping several jumps, one immediately after the other, they can lose balance and do not have time to regain it. This can lead to a rider fall and/or the horse being yanked in the mouth or the rider landing heavily on the horse's back.

There are many ways a grid can be built. The easiest grid consists of three fences, each at one non- jumping stride apart. Start with one fence, usually a cross-pole to make it inviting and keep the horse central. Asking the riders to approach in trot and land in canter will ensure they have enough impulsion for when the second fence is built. Once the horses and riders are happy going through this, set up the second fence. If there is a trot approach then 18ft/5.4m is a good starting distance for the average horse of about 15.2–16hh. Observe how the horses cope with the distance, and if it is not comfortable then be prepared to alter it. Remember the horses must approach in a forward-going trot that shows impulsion.

When horses and riders are comfortable going through the first two elements then add a third fence. This could initally be an upright, and the distance may need to be a little longer (approx. 19ft/5.8m) as the horses' frames may well be lengthening a little as they go through the grid. Again, observe whether or not the horses are finding the distance comfortable, and if not (as long as their way of going is forward and rhythmical) then move the fence to make the distance more user-friendly. A back rail could be introduced to make this fence a spread.

If the horses were to approach in canter then the distances between each fence would probably need to be 3ft/90cm longer.

Related distances:

This is where two fences are placed more than two non-jumping strides apart (which is a two-stride double), up to a distance of about 60ft/18.2m. A three-stride related distance is set at 45ft/13.7m for an easy distance. This can be a straight line or a 'dog leg'. It is no easy task to teach horses and riders to ride related distances well. The quality of the canter – rhythm, balance and length of stride – is vital, as is the line taken by the rider.

Building fences:

When building a jump always make sure that the fence does not create a false ground line for the horse. When building a fence with a 'dropper' it gives the horse a good guide if you pull the part of the pole that is on the ground forward from the wings a little towards the direction the horse is approaching from.

If there is a pole on the ground acting as a ground line, then again it makes it easier for the horse to take off at a good point if the pole is a few inches forward from the jump itself.

When building spreads for riders who are not very experienced, a cross-pole in front, rather than a straight bar, makes the fence less imposing. Also when jumping a spread that has two straight poles, making the back rail one hole higher than the front rail makes the fence more inviting (known as an ascending spread). A back rail should always be held by collapsible cups.

Never over-face a novice rider. It is always better to make the jump a little lower and put it up one hole at a time as confidence improves.

Rules of riding

- Be sure you understand the rules of use for riding areas.

  To ensure horse and rider safety it is very important that as a coach you pass on the rules for riding when in a group. It is also your responsibility to ensure that all riders in your tutelage abide by them.

  These are the accepted rules for when working in an enclosed area:

  - If working as a ride keep one horse's distance apart.

  - If working in open order pass left to left when meeting somebody who is riding at the same pace as you.

  - If riding in open order in walk then stay on an inside track leaving the track free for those going at a faster pace.

  - If riding in open order turn across the school to undertake a downwards transition.

  - If you wish to enter or leave the arena, then always ask for and obtain permission from those already there.

  - If there is anybody within the arena who is having an issue with a horse then stay well way from them at the other end of the area.

  - Jump equipment not in use should be stored neatly and safely.

  - Jump cups should not be left on wings when there are no poles on them.

  - Riding areas must be regularly maintained to ensure the surface is kept as flat as possible.

  - Cross-country jumps must be jumped the correct way round. If jumps are flagged, a red flag on the right and a white flag on the left of the jump indicate the correct direction.

  - Cross-country jumps and take-off and landing areas must be regularly maintained.

- If you have riders who want to compete you must make sure you are aware of the rules for the discipline they wish to compete in and pas these on to the riders. You must also ensure that they understand that politeness to officials and volunteers at a competition is vital if fair play is to be upheld.

How to become competent

- Learn as much as you possibly can by watching other instructors and learning from the way they use exercises to improve horses' and riders' specific problems.

- Discuss with the proprietor of your own riding school or a local school the system they use for grading riders. Some schools will try to grade according to ability, some may use age as a guide so that riders of the same peer group are riding together. Some schools may grade lessons according to the size of horse. In this case ponies would work in one ride, horses in another. This is easier when using jumping exercises (especially grids) when distances for ponies may be too short for horses.

- Be clear on the brief you would give to an assistant who was leading for you while you are giving a group lesson to beginners. Make sure they know how to hold the lead rope so that it is not uncomfortable for the horse, not wrapped round the hand, and short enough to maintain control. Remember to tell them that when they change the rein they should change sides so that they are not trapped between the wall and the horse/pony. They must realise they are responsible for control of the horse/pony and should always maintain at least one horse's distance between themselves and the horse/pony in front. When they are turned in they must make the horses stand still and be far enough from the others to be out of kicking range. Make sure they realise they are there to do as you ask and not to teach the rider.

- Speak to riders about why they have lead-rein or lunge lessons (particularly adults). Find out why riders prefer class lessons or individual lessons. Some riders like the freedom to hack, others far prefer the structure and control of riding in the school.

- Your own experiences as a rider should give you some opinions about the advantages and disadvantages of private, class, lead-rein, lunge, horse-care lessons and hacks.

- If you have the opportunity of escorting some hacks then this can be very good experience. Understand the order in which you might place the riders (e.g. less experienced or nervous closer to you), make sure you have considered the route you are taking and, if necessary, that you have a second escort to assist you. Understand your responsibilities when riding both on the road and on bridleways. Be aware of what you might take with you to ensure support in the case of an emergency (mobile phone, leaving information as to the route you are taking and approximately the time you will be away).

- If your teaching experience covers several months then you should be aware of the variation of seasonal conditions that may cause discomfort or stress in both horse and rider. Cold, wind, wet and heat can all affect the way your rider and/or horse may feel. Overworking horse or rider can also have an adverse affect.

- Be clear on how to discuss lesson plans. Watch other instructors to see how a lesson should develop. All lessons should have a period of warming up, loosening up both horse and rider and preparing them for more serious work. This period also serves to allow you to assess the rider(s) today and give you a foundation for choosing the work for the lesson. The main content of the lesson should then develop and towards the end of a lesson you should avoid starting anything new, which you may not have time to follow through to a pleasing conclusion. The lesson should have a summing up period or conclusion, where work is consolidated and the riders go away with confidence and are clear on the work covered. Always spend a little time giving the riders feedback and telling them how they will move forward in their next lesson. Ask the riders for feedback on yourself and work to take on board any constructive criticism they give.

- Make sure that you are clear on all the work that would be included in a rider's ability up to Stage 2 level and similarly consider the standard of Horse Care expected by Stage 2.

- It may not be long since you were working yourself at that level, so it should be easy for you to remember the progression of your own training to this level and feel confident about delivering a similar format to trainees working towards Stage 2.

- Make sure that you have discussed with your own trainer the options as to how and when novice riders should hold the saddle, reins or a neckstrap when learning to ride. Also watch what other instructors do in different circumstances.

- Make sure that you have watched children playing gymkhana games and generally having fun with ponies on 'own a pony day' or at pony club camp. Children get much amusement in having the opportunity to plait manes and tails, paint hooves and 'dress up' long-suffering ponies in fancy dress.

- Be careful that you can 'walk' a distance accurately, avoid talking about 'my strides'. 'Your' stride should be as near 3ft, or just under 1 metre, as possible so that you can usefully 'walk' distances accurately.

- Be confident about discussing basic distances of trotting poles (4ft 6ins/1.37m), one placing pole to a jump from a trot approach (8–9ft/2.4–2.7m), one non-jumping stride between two small fences from a trot approach (18ft/5.4m).

- The more you have experienced the exercises yourself the easier it is to visualise and help another person to develop the same skill.

- You must be able to explain the jumping position clearly and how you would teach it. You will be asked about methods to develop the rider's jumping position, and these should include practice of rhythm and pace on the flat and include poles as appropriate. You must understand and be able to explain basic jump distances (e.g. 9ft/2.7m placing pole to a jump if the approach is from trot. A canter approach to a close placing pole is not advisable for inexperienced riders).

Jumping position. The angle of the upper body can vary according to whether jumping in show-jumping or cross-country pace, as the rider's balance and ability develop.

To teach a rider to jump, the coach must be confident and competent and the horses/ponies must be used to the task and reliable. The rider must want to learn to jump; do not force anybody to jump who does not want to. They will be negative, stiff and very worried, and this could lead to an accident.

- There is no substitute for watching other teachers, learning from what they do and seeing what exercises they use for different situations.

Part C

Stages of learning, motivation, goal-setting, coaching and learning styles

How people learn

It is generally agreed that there are four stages of learning:

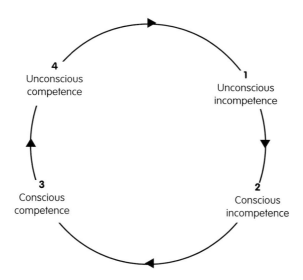

If we take an example of a person wishing to learn to ride:

Often those who have never ridden think it is easy to do so and they can just 'get on and do it'. This is unconscious incompetence. They are unaware of what is involved in the basics of riding and how difficult it is to stay balanced and use the most basic of aids.

On getting onto a horse the first few times they become aware of what is involved and realise that they are unable to make a horse do what they want to do. This is conscious incompetence. They realise how many skills are involved and that there is much to learn.

They start to learn skills of using their aids, staying in balance and reacting to the horse they are riding. They have to think carefully about what they are doing and work hard to learn the new skills required. This is conscious competence.

As their skills improve they are able to use them without thinking and can start, stop and turn with ease. They have now reached the stage of unconscious competence. Once this stage of learning is reached then the rider will be able to move on and learn other new skills through the same process. For instance, once they have mastered the basic aids they may well start to learn to jump or move on to more complicated flatwork.

As a coach you must remember that many of your personal riding skills will probably be at the unconscious competence stage. You must remember that your learners will not be at this stage and will still have many difficulties to overcome. It is a major part of your role to understand this and find ways to help them overcome their issues so that they achieve their goals, enjoy riding and want to continue in their sport.

When teaching new exercises it is important to remember the phases of learning. Different learning styles (see pages 102 to 104) must also be taken into consideration.

You must ensure that riders have the level of competence necessary to learn a new skill. For example, it is no use trying to teach a rider about their diagonals when they are not competent in rising trot. For them to have to concentrate on how to rise and work out which pair of legs to rise on at the same time would overload them. This would lead to them being unsuccessful and possibly de-motivated.

Many people will learn something new if they can understand the reason why they need to learn it. So, when explaining a fresh topic, try to put in simple language why there is a necessity to learn the skill. It is very important that any explanation is put into language that is suitable for the riders you are teaching. Children will respond better to simple language that is couched in terms they understand.

After the explanation of the new skill it is important that there is a demonstration of some kind – maybe a member of the group is used, or the coach may demonstrate. It is important to encourage the riders to ask questions to ensure they understand. An open question such as, 'How are you going to attempt this?' is much more useful than a closed question (i.e. one leading to a yes or no answer) such as, 'Do you understand?'

Once the new skill has been explained and demonstrated then there has to be plenty of time for practising. As previously mentioned with such a practical topic there is no substitute for being 'hands on'. The coach may have to find several different ways of presenting the same skill. The riders will then not lose interest and will persevere until the skill is learnt. Throughout the process the riders should be encouraged to discuss what they are feeling and thinking, and be helped to work through any issues they have. When riders are engaged in their learning they will learn more quickly and will better retain the knowledge and skill.

Motivation

There are many definitions of motivation, but generally it can be said to be the driver that makes us want to do something. If we are not motivated then we will not want to do something and so will not be successful. For many people riding is a hobby and something to be enjoyed. If it is not enjoyable then there will be no motivation to continue. Many people give up riding because they lose their motivation. As coaches it is important to understand what is motivating our riders. If we can keep motivation high then we will keep them riding. In a commercial situation this is vital to ensure viability as well as to help riders find and keep the same pleasure we get from riding.

There are two forms of motivation:

Extrinsic

This form of motivation comes from outside ourselves. It can be from parents, peers, outside agencies and can also include circumstances, situations, rewards or punishments.

With children you may well find that there is a great deal of extrinsic motivation. Parents may well be pushing a child to ride when they do not particularly want to, or they may be trying to push the child to progress too fast. This is a tricky situation that, if identified, may best be dealt with by the most senior member of staff at an establishment. A tactful discussion with the parents may be the best solution.

In a class situation a child could feel peer pressure to try an exercise that they are not happy with. This is one of the reasons that all exercises within a session must be set at a level that suits the least proficient rider. Peer pressure on young people in all walks of life leads to huge issues for children and if we, within riding, can start to make children aware of the fact that they are all individuals in their own right and help to give them self-confidence then we may well be influencing their development in many areas.

Intrinsic

Intrinsic motivation comes from the inside. It stems from what we want to do. If we do not have intrinsic motivation to achieve something then it is highly unlikely that it will be successful over the long term.

It is important to try and find out what is motivating your riders. You will then be able to utilise this in your coaching, helping them to improve and stay focused. You also need to find out what they find de-motivating, for example, they might not enjoy riding a particular horse or being pushed out of their comfort zone.

Goal setting

It is important for us to have goals to know where we want to get to and to use as a bench-mark to tell if we have been successful.

A rider can have:

- A 'dream golden goal', e.g. 'I want to win a gold medal at the Olympics of 2016.'

- A long-term goal, e.g. 'I want to compete at Badminton in 2014.'

- A short-term goal, e.g. 'I want to improve the quality of my horse's canter by the end of the month.'

- A session goal, e.g. 'I want to improve the stability of my lower leg over a fence in today's session.'

All goals should be **SMART**:

Specific

Measurable

Achievable

Realistic

Time related

A dream goal may be just that, but it may help to plan out your long-term, short-term and session goals.

Although the example goals above may not be realistic for the weekly rider it is still important for them to set goals. You as the coach should assist in ensuring they are SMART.

All goals should aim to balance challenge and stress to aid development.

Your weekly rider may have a long-term goal of being able to hack out safely by the spring, a short-term goal of learning to jump a single fence by the end of the month, and a single session goal of being able to get the correct canter lead every time they ask for it in the session. These all provide a structure and enable planning and give both you and the rider something to gauge improvements by.

Coaching Styles

How do you coach your clients? Take a few minutes to think about this. Do you always coach in the same way or do you adapt the way in which you conduct a session depending on who you are working with?

Generally there are three agreed coaching styles:

Autocratic

i. Telling: The coach decides on what is to be done. The riders are not involved in the decision making. The coach defines what to do and how to do it.

ii. Selling: The coach decides on what is to be done. The coach explains what is required and the objectives. The riders are encouraged to ask questions to confirm understanding. The coach defines what to do and how to do it.

Democratic:

i. Sharing: The coach outlines the training requirements to the riders. The coach invites ideas/suggestions from the riders. The coach makes the decision based on the riders' suggestions. The coach defines what to do and how to do it.

ii. Allowing: The coach outlines the training requirements to the riders. The coach defines the training conditions. The riders brainstorm to explore possible solutions. The riders make the decision. The riders define what to do and how to do it.

Laissez Faire:

There is little direction from a laissez faire coaching style as this style allows the group to do what they want to and coaches coach from what is seen.

Coaches will use a variety of styles/types depending on the coaching situation.

In days gone by the majority of riding teaching has been autcratic telling. There is still a place for this method of coaching especially with a group of novice riders whose safety needs to be assured. They can still, however, be engaged in a session and asked for feedback on what they are feeling and how everything is going. Where a rider is very experienced and working towards something specific there may be a more democratic sharing coaching style. As a coach it is important to be flexible in your approach and be able to use whichever style is appropriate for those you are helping. This is no easy feat when you are just starting in your coaching career, but should certainly be a part of your personal long term action plan.

Learning Styles

Everybody learns in a slightly different way and it is important for coaches to recognise this and try to adapt what they are teaching so that riders have an opportunity to learn better and more quickly.

There are two principle model theories about how people learn. The first by Honey and Mumford highlights four different ways people learn:

i. An activist is a person who likes to learn by doing things, trying them out, act first and consider the consequences afterwards. They become bored when they have to listen to long explanations and have to follow instructions to the letter.

ii. A reflector likes to stand back and think about experiences, observe them first and then review what has happened. They do not learn well when they have no time to prepare, are thrown in at the deep end and are rushed.

iii. A theorist tends to be a perfectionist who likes to think things through and analyse them. They like logic and to be given the chance to question and probe ideas. They do not learn well when an activity is unstructured and they have to do things without knowing the principles or concepts involved.

iv. A pragmatist is keen to try out new ideas, theories and techniques to see if they work. They like to copy a model and look for techniques where an obvious advantage is shown to them. They learn less well when no immediate benefit can be recognised, there is no apparent payback to the learning and no practice or guidelines are given.

The second theory highlights three different ways people learn and is known as VAK:

i.   A Visual learner learns by looking at things.

ii. An Auditory learner learns by listening.

iii. A Kinaesthetic learner learns by doing.

People may well not learn utilising only one of these styles but may employ something from each of them. Throughout their life their style may well change. Many young people nowadays know their preferred learning style as they will undertake a simple exercise at school. If you wish to find out you and your clients preferred style then there are numerous simple tests on the internet that you can download to utilise. It is important for you to recognise your own preferred style. This can then assist you to communicate with those you coach. It can also help you to understand why sometimes people do not relate to what you are trying to teach them. Try to ensure you find different techniques for teaching so that all your clients can relate to what you are trying to help them learn. For instance in teaching diagonals you might give a description first, then demonstrate (possibly with different coloured bandages on the horse's diagonal legs), give riders time to reflect and ask questions and then allow them to practise. In class lessons it can be difficult to ensure you cater for all learning styles, but with imagination and experience you will be able to do this.

It must be remembered that children and adults learn in different ways.

Children need to have fun while they are learning and need lots of encouragement and positive feedback. Children mature and develop at a different pace to their chronological peers and this must be taken into consideration. Children tend to have a shorter attention span than adults and so sessions must be structured so that their interest is kept.

Adults may want more in-depth information about what they are doing and be happy to practice the same thing over and over to ensure they have learnt. They may ask more in-depth questions than children and want to be given a guide as to where they can research further what they have learnt in their session.

It is easier to start to get adults to take responsibility for their own learning by questioning them and getting them to give you feedback. Children should also be encouraged to give you feedback, but it may well not be in so much depth.

What the assessor is looking for

- You may be asked about goal setting and these questions are likely to come in the theory/discussion part of the examination. They may also be touched on when discussing your practical sessions.

- You should be able to explain why a lesson should have an aim or goal.

- Understand that a pupil learning any subject will be able to prepare and plan their development more easily if they have clear aims or goals set out for them.

- Understand that goals may be golden, long-term, short-term or sessional.

- Be able to discuss how these goals may be chosen for each rider.

- Consider what a sessional goal might be in a one-hour class lesson of weekly riders (e.g. today we are going to start to learn about diagonals in trot, by the end of the lesson we will aim to have you understanding what diagonals are and how you recognise which one you are riding on).

- Consider and be able to discuss some long-term goals (e.g. by the end of the summer holidays we will aim for you being able to jump a small course of fences).

- Be able to discuss how goals might change. (A long-term goal may be for the rider to enter a competition in six months' time.) A long-term goal may have to change if a rider misses riding due to an unexpected illness or progresses more quickly than anticipated when the goal was set. The goal may then be moved forward or back from the original time scale planned.

- Be able to discuss motivation or enthusiasm to progress.

- Understand and be able to talk about what motivates a rider (seeing other members of the peer group progressing, friends or family inspiring the rider, having a clear goal to aim for).

- Motivation is a moveable and fragile state, which can be influenced by good or bad teaching, by a good or bad experience on the horse.

- Riders can be self-motivated or at times need to be motivated by others.

- Be aware of different coaching styles and where and when they may be relevant.

How to become competent

- Consider what goals you have set yourself, or had set for you, during your life but particularly with regard to your riding career.

- Goals must be appropriate and realistic for the rider concerned, they must be achievable and measurable. If they are not any of these things, then often they are unachievable and this in itself can be very demotivating if a goal is unattainable.

- Consider other trainers of riders and consider how they establish goals and what those goals are.

- Watch the outcome of the goal setting and realise that there are times when a goal may have to be adjusted (up or down) to take account of a change in circumstances (e.g. a horse goes lame and then a competition, which was planned, may have to be rescheduled or abandoned).

- Goal setting and motivation have some connection. Recognise that achieving a goal for a rider is very motivating and at that point a new goal should be set to keep the rider's interest and commitment.

- Ask riders (both those you may teach yourself and others) what drives them; find out what stimulates their enthusiasm.

- Also find out what lowers their motivation. It may be things like the winter, cold dark nights, and lack of someone with whom to share their interest.

- Watching top riders on television or video may motivate riders. Talking to other riders and sharing similar experiences may stimulate them.

- Try to watch lessons as often as you can and consider what the short-term goal might be for that lesson, whether it was clear at the beginning and whether it was achieved.

- Ask other instructors to clarify their sessional, short and long-term goals with a group of riders or an individual.

- Analyse your own coaching style and try to utilise other coaching styles at appropriate times.

Part D

Safety

When coaching riders safety must be your first priority. Clients put their faith in you and you should respect that by doing everything you can to ensure the safety of both them and the horses they are riding. Many basic safety precautions have already been discussed throughout this book.

One way to make certain that safety is kept as a priority is to ensure that the behaviour of your riders is managed well and that ground rules are laid down. Riders should sign to say they agree to the Code of Conduct that the centre has lain down and parents should be aware that if children do not behave they will be asked to leave the premises. Besides helping to keep sessions safe rules also prevent time wasting and loss of focus.

To encourage riders to behave in a positive manner you, the coach, must treat them all with respect and speak to them in a polite manner. As the coach you should set a good example to riders and others to act as a role model for good behaviour. Positive behaviour, especially in children and young people, should be praised.

All lessons should have a risk assessment undertaken to ensure that all potential risks and hazards have been considered. The easiest way to undertake a risk assessment is to break down the lesson into sections/exercises, write them down and then consider the potential risks and hazards. Grade the risks 1, 2 or 3 and do the same for the hazards. If you multiply these two numbers together you will know how high the potential risk is. Within the risk assessment you must also note what you are going to do to minimise the risk.

Your experience coaching and round the yard will help you with highlighting where the high risk issues are. By discussing them with other involved parties (e.g. clients and helpers) you are already starting to minimise the risk.

Although it is essential to try and minimise the risk, there will occasionally be times when the unexpected occurs. It is essential that the coach has a knowledge of accident procedure. Whether it is in a ride or on the yard, the basic process is the same:

BHS RISK ASSESSMENT

ACTIVITY ASSESSED

Hazard and severity (1 = minor, 2 = serious, 3 = very serious/fatal)

Risk (likelihood) (1= very unlikely, 2 = unlikely, 3 = likely/very likely)

Hazard x Risk = Hazard severity (1–3 = low, 4 or 5 = medium, 6+ = high)

HAZARD	AT RISK	CONTROLS	RISK RATING (RR)	OTHER PRECAUTIONS

Firstly, stay calm and assess the situation. Never put yourself or others at further risk if an accident has occurred. There is no point in ending up with extra casualties.

Secondly, assess the casualty. Make sure they are not in any secondary danger. Talk to them as you approach. If they are crying or screaming that is better than them being silent. If they are silent they may be unconscious.

If they are still and silent, send somebody else to dial 999 (in the UK) and call an ambulance. Meanwhile you should go up to the casualty and check for a response. Call their name and give them a gentle shake on the shoulder.

Remember ABC:

- **Airway**: Open and clear the airway. Tilt the person's head backwards by lifting the chin up and supporting the head with your other hand. If they are wearing their riding hat, do not remove it. Check there are no obstructions in the mouth. This can range from false teeth to the tongue having slipped back.

- **Breathing**: Check that the casualty is still breathing. Do this by placing your ear near their mouth or check their ribcage for movement up and down. If they are not breathing you need to undertake CPR, for which you need specialist training. (If you have attended a BHS First Aid Course or a four-day Health and Safety at Work Course, you will have practised these skills.)

- **Circulation**: Check the casualty still has a pulse by pressing two fingers on the carotid artery, which can be found by the windpipe on the neck. It is a good idea to practise finding this pulse on yourself so you know exactly where to feel for it on a casualty.

Keep the casualty warm until professional help arrives. Do not move the casualty unless you have to leave them alone. (The only time you would need to do this is if there is nobody else around and you have to leave to summon professional help. If this situation does arise then place the casualty in the 'recovery position'. This position ensures that the airway cannot become blocked.) It is important to only use the recovery position when absolutely necessary as moving the casualty could cause further issues if a spinal injury is involved.

If the casualty is conscious, assess the situation before making any decisions on what to do. It is important to keep the casualty still and talk to them to give reassurance. Ensure, by observing them, that they are not having any breathing difficulties. If there is an obvious major injury then send somebody to dial 999 for professional assistance. While you are waiting, if the casualty is bleeding then try and stem this by applying direct pressure. If an arm or a leg is bleeding then raising the limb above the level of the heart can slow this. If a limb appears to be at a peculiar angle or there is an obvious broken bone, then make every effort to keep the person still so that the issue is not compounded. Keep the casualty warm. Be self-assured to give the casualty and other people confidence.

It is absolutely vital that after every incident you fill out an accident report form or the accident/incident book as per the policy of the yard. If the casualty is a child then an insurance claim can be made up to three years after their 18th birthday. This could be a good many years, so accurate information is imperative. All the details should be recorded: date, time, names of rider and horse, exercises being undertaken and general facts about the incident. The weather should also be noted as should the names and contact details of any witnesses. Insurers advise centres not to take statements from witnesses, but to leave that task to them should the necessity arise. The insurers will then ensure that the language used by witnesses is not derogatory to the incident.

Any accident that involves a broken bone (other than a finger or toe) or hospitalisation, has to be reported to the local Environmental Health Department through RIDDOR.

What the assessor is looking for (safety)

- The most important thing is to appear confident about what you should and should not do. The assessor would like to feel as if you were helping the situation, not exacerbating the issue.

- You must be able to talk confidently about basic care of casualties.

- You must stress the importance of calling for professional help.

- Remember to discuss the importance of accident reporting, what needs to be written down and why.

How to become competent (safety)

- The best way to become competent is to take either the BHS First Aid course or the four-day Health and Safety at Work course.

- Ask if you can read the accident report book to understand how to fill one in.

- Discuss the RIDDOR process with your proprietor.

Why is Child Protection an issue?

- High physical risks
- Close proximity of instructors
- Physical contact
- Competitive atmosphere/pressure
- Elite athletes higher risk of abuse
- Can aid child protection because of possible close relationships forged

Who needs to be protected

- Children
- Riders with disabilities
- Riding instructors
- Volunteers

How can we protect them?

- British Equestrian Federation (BEF) Child Protection Policy
- BHS Instructors Register and Code of Conduct
- Good Practice
- Risk Assessment
- Safe recruitment procedures
- Training
- Accurate record keeping

Good Practice

- Ensure experience at equestrian events is fun and enjoyable
- Be an excellent role model
- Ensure that the training and competition intensity is appropriate to the physical and emotional development of the rider
- Conduct training and meetings in an open environment and avoid one-to-one coaching in unobserved situations
- Avoid unnecessary physical contact

Poor Practice

- Never take children to your home where they will be alone with you
- Never allow children to use inappropriate language unchallenged

Physical contact after a fall:

Get down to their level, check they are unhurt, and then, facing them, hold their hands in yours, look them in the eyes, squeeze their hands and reassure them it is alright and that everything is OK.

This is the safest and best method and is recommended by Sports Coach UK and the NSPCC.

Recognising Abuse

Physical signs

- Bruising
- Injuries
- Weight loss/gain
- Inadequate clothing, poor personal hygiene

Behavioural signs

- Aggression
- Introversion
- Low self esteem
- Delayed development
- Self harm

Incident reporting

Responding to the child

- Create a safe environment
- Be honest, never promise to keep secrets
- Record all the facts
- Maintain confidentiality but do not take on sole responsibility

Responding to allegations

- Discuss concerns with parents or carers
- Consult a senior collegue
- Consult/inform Governing Body Child Protection Officer (CPO)
- Inform social services/police
- Obtain medical attention
- Record everything

Clubmark

Background information

Clubmark is a mark of high quality clubs which helps to reassure parents, participants and local authorities that the club serves its participants well. Sports clubs that work with children and young people need and deserve support to improve the quality of work they do.

Benefits to clubs:

Its benefits include club development, increased membership, developing coaches and volunteers and an increased profile. The legitimacy to work with local authorities and other government agencies will also be enabled.

Benefits to participants

- Ensure the well-being of young people whilst in the care of adults, other than their legal parent(s)/carer(s)
- Enthuse young people to enjoy sport and active recreation to build a healthy and active lifestyle
- Enable young people to use their leisure time creatively
- Allow young people to optimise their talents and personal ability
- Identify and support the development of the most talented young people

What does it include

Clubmark accreditation involves completing a portfolio, which includes four sections plus an action plan:

- The Playing Programme
- Duty of care and child protection
- Sports equity and ethics
- Club management
- Action plan

Gathering the evidence is straightforward; each club is allocated a Clubmark officer and an assessor. The Clubmark officer will be there to support the club throughout the accreditation.

Further information

www.clubmark.org.uk
www.bhs.org.uk

What the assessor is looking for

- You should know that under a duty of care, you as the instructor in charge, should show a responsibility throughout all your time when working with clients for their safety and well-being.

- You will ensure that at all times you work in the best interests of the clients' safety. (You ensure that they have help if needed with the horse they are leading/riding/mounting etc.)

- You understand that good practice is your ability to give a well-planned, well-delivered, clear lesson according to the needs of your pupil(s) whom you will have assessed.

- Good practice follows a safe code of behaviour based on good judgement and awareness of your pupil(s)' needs.

- You never choose work which they would not be capable of carrying out (which would endanger them). Poor practice would jeopardise your pupil(s)' safety and well-being.

- Be able to consider what indications there may be of abuse. The child may lose weight, may be more aggressive or tearful, there may be signs of physical bruising, this may be apparent if in the summer the child is in a short-sleeved shirt.

- Understand that your first responsibility is for the welfare of the child, but you must approach the issue with great sensitivity.

- Always refer in the first instance to the senior member of staff to whom you are responsible.

- Beware of making any accusations without sufficient evidence, and even then be very careful to have a witness with you in the event that such discussion is not constructively received.

- You should be aware of the BEF incident reporting procedure which is available from the BEF Safeguarding Children and Vulnerable Adults Manual.

How to become competent

- Listen and learn, ask advice from other more senior instructors.

- Attend a safeguarding children and vulnerable adults course, run by the BHS (see appendix) where you will receive training on how to recognise and deal with children who might be suffering verbal, physical or emotional abuse from an adult.

- Consider the code of practice that exists in the establishment in which you teach or use the BEF code of practice.

- Consider how you should follow that code of good practice and conversely what would be considered as poor practice (e.g. good practice ensures that riders are never asked to attempt anything of which they are not capable or of which they feel apprehensive).

- Poor practice could be considered if a beginner rider were to be taken hacking and riding along a main road when their balance and coordination was barely established, and the instructor was chatting to her friend and using a mobile phone, with little or no regard for her pupil. (This scenario would completely lack good judgement and therefore the outcome would be poor practice.)

- Bear in mind that abuse could be considered if a rider were to be pressurised into working harder than their physical fitness allowed (e.g. if a beginner rider were to be expected to work for an entire lesson in trot without stirrups).

PTT

Portfolio
Building

Portfolio Building

When you register for the PTT you will be sent a portfolio which you can work to complete. You can start to work on the portfolio before you take your PTT and certain work you undertake to prepare for your PTT forms an integral part of the document. You will also have the opportunity to register for the United Kingdom Coaching Certificate Endorsed Level 2 in Coaching. If you register for your UKCC Level 2 then the portfolio you receive will have more parts to complete.

The portfolio comes with concise instructions on how to complete all the sections and as to who can sign off the various sections. It also contains a number of appendices which can be used as proformas for the work you have to complete.

There are three parts to the portfolio. In **part one** of the portfolio you are required to:

Plan and prepare a series of four linked coaching sessions.

1. Identify, evaluate and record the needs of the rider(s) that you intend to coach.

For this you can use the rider registration form which is Appendix 1 in the portfolio or the rider registration form from your centre. There should be a copy for each of the riders in the group of four you are coaching. If you coach individuals there should be one for each of four separate riders.

You should black out their personal details before putting the sheets in the portfolio.

From this information you can analyse the needs of the riders and record them on a coaching participant record sheet. Again you should blank out their personal details and there should be a copy for each of your riders.

You need to produce four horse suitability profiles – one for each rider.

2. Produce coaching plans for the four linked riding sessions.

This is an outlined plan for the four linked sessions and should show that

- you have considered the resources that are required

- there is a logical duration and sequence for each session

- there is a suitable degree of intensity for each session

- you have considered your mode of delivery

- the technical content for each session is suitable.

You should then write a comprehensive session plan for each of the four individual sessions making it clear how you intend to break down the delivery of each session, identifying the aim of each of the activities that are going to be undertaken.

3. You need to show evidence that you have planned for a safe coaching environment for each session.

For this you need to produce a risk assessment for each session.

4. You must show you have evaluated your coaching practice for each of the 4 sessions by completing four self-evaluations.

Part two of the portfolio consists of the paperwork from your PTT exam. Your lesson plans and risk assessments and the formal assessment which will be completed at the PTT exam; the paperwork from this needs to be put into the portfolio after the exam. The coach candidate report, will be completed by the assessor on the day of your exam and will be sent to you with the results. The self-evaluation of coaching and personal action plan will be completed by yourself and the assessor on the day and, again , will be sent to you from Stoneleigh with your results.

Part three of the portfolio is a professional and personal development form which is there to help you progress.

A copy of your PTT certificate should also be placed in the portfolio.

If you are using the portfolio to gain your BHSAI you must also place copies of your

Stage 1,2, and 3 Horse Knowledge, Care and Riding in the portfolio along with a copy of the relevant first aid qualification and certificate of attendance from a Safeguarding and Protecting Children workshop.

If you register for the UKCC level 2 then the work discussed above has to be completed. There are also other exercises that need to be undertaken to complete the portfolio.

PTT
Questions and Answers

The following are some basic answers to typical questions that assessors may ask.

- Remember that the questions are given as a guide only.

- Be confident that you can answer any question.

- Be sure that you have considered all the questions and feel able to add a little more information to each rather than just the minimal answer that is offered. The answer offered is to encourage you to do your own further research and to be able to expand your ideas on all subjects.

Q. A new client phones for information and to book a lesson. What information do you need to give? What information do you require from him/her?

A. Information you need to give:

What time lessons run.

How long the lesson is.

How much the lesson costs.

The number of riders in a lesson.

The standard of instructor taking the lesson.

The range of lesson types (lunge, lead-rein, class, private etc.).

The location of the establishment.

Specific information relevant to assessing new riders and introductory lessons to acquaint the new client with the centre.

Information from the client:

Past riding history, if any.

Age if under 18 (and approximately if adult).

Approximate height and weight.

What type of lesson they wish to take.

Q. Discuss ways of running an office regarding bookings, allocation of horses/ponies, payment and how it is recorded.

A. Here it may be appropriate to discuss the specific system that you have used in an establishment where you have worked or trained. E.g. Bookings taken by the secretary or person manning the office; liaison between the person running the office and the instructional staff to ensure that lessons are not overbooked; a senior member of the teaching staff who can mount clients according to their ability and standard of the lesson to make horse/pony allocation; payment made when the client arrives and record made in the day book with a forward booking taken at that time if required, etc.

Q. How do you encourage new clients to become regular clients?

A. Run a welcoming and friendly establishment.

Have horses/ponies that are gentle, pleasant to handle and well-schooled to ride.

Give encouraging lessons which stimulate fun, enthusiasm and learning.

Encourage groups of like-minded people of similar standard to ride together.

Offer incentives to riders to book ahead and arrange lessons in advance with a discount or free lesson for booking a number at a time.

Run any kind of social activity (school outing to Badminton) so that riders feel part of the establishment.

Q. What clothing is essential for beginner riders and how long would it be before you expected correct riding attire?

A. Safe footwear (sturdy shoes with a heel, not a ridged sole and preferably lace-up or zip shoes or boots – not trainers or wellingtons).

Trousers which are comfortable and not too tight-fitting.

No loose clothing, fashion clothing or jewellery.

Preferably gloves and a warm waterproof coat if outdoors and winter.

Correctly fitting riding hat which complies with current BSI standards for safety. (Possible to hire or borrow one from the establishment.)

Gradually clients should be encouraged to own their own riding attire, starting with a hat.

Q. What is your policy when clients arrive unsuitably clothed or wearing jewellery?

A. If the school policy of advising clients before they arrive has been applied then it should not arise. If a client is unsafely dressed then this must be pointed out. It should be pointed out that excessive jewellery (dangling ear rings, bracelets etc.) might be damaged or lost or could be a danger to the rider if it became caught (on this basis it is advisable to remove it). Basic safety – as in hat, shoes and trousers – must be adhered to in the interests of everyone's well-being.

Q. If lending BSI approved hats or body protectors to clients, what advice would you give on how they should fit?

A. Advise that you are not a qualified fitter. Advise that the hat/body protector should fit comfortably and stay in place without the person having to worry about it. Advise that the ultimate responsibility is with them to feel happy with the equipment and, if in doubt, they should provide their own.

Q. A new client wants to go for a hack and not have a lesson. Your policy is to assess everyone in a school or arena before allowing them to hack. How do you handle the situation?

A. Advise that the policy of the school is to assess and that it is for the benefit of the clients to ensure that they are safe to hack. Be polite but do not deviate from your rule, emphasising that your insurance policy requires that you are only able to allow clients to hack if they are deemed of a standard that the school has assessed as capable. A new client whether they are for lessons or hacking out must always complete a rider registration form.

Q. How many riders would you have in a class lesson? Does this depend on their standard? Would you use assistants or helpers and how would you brief them prior to the lesson?

A. A class lesson where much individual attention can be given consisting of four, six or eight riders is practical and increasingly viable economically.

Helpers can be an asset, particularly with novice riders or children who may need to be led or may need some individual help within the class. The helpers must be briefed to look to the coach for exact information throughout the lesson, according to the circumstances that arise.

Q. Is it practical to 'grade' riders so that class lessons contain riders of similar standards? Discuss and give the advantages and disadvantages.

A. It is usually an advantage to grade riders for class lessons. This enables riders to progress at a similar rate and is easier for the coach to manage. Some riders may still progress faster in spite of this policy, but this can provide an inspiration to others to try harder. Mixed ability rides are more difficult to teach to keep everyone challenged at their level and happy with their progress.

Q. Are children's holiday courses a good idea? Discuss.

A. Generally, yes. The children progress by spending a week handling, tacking up, riding and being around the pony/horse for a concentrated time. It is easy to progress to fun activities such as gymkhana games, handy pony competition and fancy dress, things that there would not be time for in usual weekly lessons. There does need to be an adequate number of staff to cover these courses.

Q. What is meant by lesson structure?

A. A lesson that has a structure, has an aim, an introduction to that aim, a period of assessment and working-in when a choice is made on how to move the lesson forward. The lesson then has a period of work to develop the aim following through into a conclusion where the aim of the lesson is consolidated and the riders go away with confidence in what they have covered. During the conclusion there should be a summing up of the lesson and a plan for future lessons or some pointers to take away for the rider to think about or if possible work on for the future.

Q. How would your teaching differ for adults and children?

A. Children have a much shorter attention span.

Children have little inbuilt fear or anxiety about what 'might' happen so tend to be much more trusting of your expertise.

125

Children may be physically or mentally immature in their ability to control the pony/horse.

Adults tend to want to know more of the 'why' in doing things.

Adults have a greater awareness of 'how far it is to the ground!'

Adults may be physically less agile and supple.

Q. How would you prefer to start beginner riders? Lead rein, lunge, class, etc.

A. Lead rein is often good for small children where the contact is closer with the control of the horse/pony being taken by the leader. Very nervous adults will also benefit from lead rein lessons.

Lunge enables the teacher to have control of the horse but a good view of their pupil and the pupil can take some control of the horse as instructed. Some beginners find it hard to relax on the lunge.

Class lessons enable pupils to learn from each other and to gain confidence from each other.

Class lessons are more economically viable for a riding school.

Lunge lessons are labour intensive (one instructor/one pupil) and intensive on the horse.

Lead-rein lessons can be run with competent leaders under the control of one instructor.

Q. What teaching aids would you like to have available for lessons and lectures?

A. Cones, poles, small jumps (plastic jump blocks) for lessons.

Flip chart, white/black board, video, DVD. Good training books.

Q. How can lessons be kept interesting when the weather is bad and only a school or a manege is available for several months?

A. Involve the riders in pony/horse management sessions, grooming and tacking up prior to a lesson can teach stable-care skills and warm the riders up on a cold day.

Gymkhana games and 'handy' pony/horse exercises and gymnastic pole and jump work can all add to lesson variety.

Q. How can clients who prefer to hack out be encouraged to join lessons when the weather is too bad for hacking – and likely to be for some time due to ground conditions?

A. Run a simple competition within the school for clients in a basic riding (competence) test, basic stable management (perhaps some turn-out and plaiting) and encourage all clients to 'have a go'; this will encourage those who only hack to take some interest in the 'learning' of riding and care skills.

Have some kind of achievement badge, award, star system for clients who take a number of riding or stable management lessons.

Work clients towards the BHS Progressive Riding tests in the establishment.

Q. Exercises have to be taught and carried out well to be of benefit. Give examples.

A. Teaching basic school figures e.g. 20m circle and three-loop serpentine both require that the instructor shows the pupil clearly where the figure goes in the school. Using cones or markers to indicate the four points of a circle, or the points in the arena where the loops will pass, then enables the riders to ride accurately and they can then concentrate on the energy to sustain the pace and the rhythm of the gait.

The instructor may demonstrate himself or use one competent member of the class to show the rest of the class how an exercise should be ridden.

Q. When lungeing a rider what guidelines would you give as to holding – the reins (contact or not) the saddle, the neckstrap?

A. The rider should learn from the very first lesson how to hold the reins (as the reins are an essential part of the rider's aids and coordination so cannot be introduced too early).

At first the rider should learn to hold the reins with a fairly slack contact (leader or lunger will be in control of the horse). If necessary until they have their balance they can rest their hands on or hold the saddle at the same time.

Gradually the rider should be able to hold the reins and let go of the saddle first with one hand, then the other, then with both hands (first in walk only, then in trot).

The neckstrap should be there as a last resort, a 'grab' handle (rather than the horse's mouth).

Q. Explain what you mean by – and how you teach: half halt, turns and circles, impulsion, balance, diagonals, transitions, suppleness, forwardness, self-carriage, outline.

All these need careful study and understanding and the answers given below will only provide the briefest snapshot of a full answer.

A. **Half halt** is a preparatory aid which warns the horse of a further aid to come (e.g. half halt before riding a canter transition to warn the horse of the impending aid to canter). Teaching a rider about the half halt evolves through the rider's ability to 'prepare to' do something and by this apply their legs into a mildly containing hand which puts the horse's hocks under him and makes him more able to respond to the next aid.

Turns and circles. A turn is a change of direction through a 45-degree or 90-degree turn, a circle is a curved line sustaining a size of circle from 20m down to 15, 10 and 8m. The aids for a turn and a circle are similar; the aids for a turn are applied and then released after the turn, whereas the aids for a circle are applied for the duration of riding the circle (inside rein gives direction, inside leg maintains energy, outside rein controls the pace and the degree of bend and the outside leg controls the hindquarters with a position a little behind the girth).

Impulsion is contained or stored energy. The rider learns to generate the energy through the legs and a secure position is sustained through the seat and then they can regulate the energy they have created through their rein aids.

Balance is the horse's ability to carry his own weight and that of his rider over his four legs in whatever pace or movement is required of him to enable him to move with maximum ease and efficiency. Learning about balance comes with time and practice and developing feel for the horse underneath you.

Diagonals relate to the rider's position in rising trot relevant to the diagonal movement of the horse's legs. The rider must learn to recognise and ride on both diagonals in order to balance the horse on both reins in trot work. Developing the rider's awareness of diagonals is taught over a period of time and is easiest to start in walk, where the rider has time to watch the horse's shoulders moving forwards and backwards. As the shoulder moves back the foot is on the floor, as the shoulder moves forward, the foot is in the air. Transferring this to trot enables the rider to see which foreleg is on the ground as they sit in the saddle. If the left shoulder is coming back as the rider sits in the rising trot then the rider is sitting on the left diagonal. If the rider sits one extra beat in the trot they automatically change diagonal. This process takes time, patience and practice.

Transitions are changes of pace from a slower to a faster pace, from a faster to a slower pace or changes within a pace. They require preparation, clearly applied aids and a developing awareness of timing for the feel of the horse's balance. They are fundamental in the development of rider skill and the correct development of the horse's training.

Suppleness evolves from the horse's correct training and a harmony and balance in the way the rider rides the horse and communicates with him. Suppleness is impeded by a poorly balanced or uncoordinated rider.

Forwardness also evolves from correct training and riding. A horse that is trained to be responsive to the rider's aids and a rider who rides in balance and harmony will produce a situation where the horse is willing to go forward because it is easy for him to do so.

Self-carriage evolves from the horse's ability to carry himself correctly and in balance and with forwardness and suppleness.

Outline relates to the shape of the horse from his croup to his poll. It should be a rounded profile of a convex nature. The hind legs step under the horse, his back is rounded and forming a supple bridge between the activity of the hind legs, the carriage of the neck up from the shoulder and a submissive relaxed contact of the mouth through the elasticity of the poll and the jaw.

Q. What do you mean by jumping position or balanced seat when jumping? How do you develop it when teaching?

A. Adopting jumping position teaches riders a position which will help them to be in balance when the horse goes through the five phases of a jump (approach, take off, in the air, landing, getaway). The rider adapts his or her position to be able to stay in harmony with the horse as the horse changes his balance through these phases.

The rider adopts a slightly shorter stirrup length (one or two holes) and is then able to close the angles in the joints between foot and lower leg, lower leg and thigh and thigh and upper body. In this more closed position and taking the shoulders forward with a slightly shorter rein, the rider's seat moves back in the saddle and the rider covers a broader more flexible base position in the saddle, the seat is lighter and more weight is taken into the lower leg and heel which is deep and flexible. The rider is in a secure position to move in balance with the horse as he jumps.

The rider should work in jumping position in walk, trot and canter and over poles to establish confidence and security in this position before starting to jump.

Q. What are the advantages of using a grid?

(a) For horses

A. It develops the horse's confidence and athleticism in jumping. It can develop his suppleness in dealing with different distances.

(b) For riders

A. It develops the rider's confidence and ability while not having to worry about the distance between fences. It can bring the rider into exactly the right position for the jumps.

Q. Give examples of distances for trotting poles and various ways of using them to the benefit of horse and rider.

A. Poles would usually be set at 4ft 6in (1.35m); these would be appropriate for trotting. Poles can be set singly or in groups of three or more to improve the rider's balance and accuracy to ride to the centre. The horse is improved in his early training in work over poles to develop, rhythm, balance and confidence.

Canter poles can also be used for more experienced horses and riders (set between 9ft/2.7m and 12ft/3.6m).

(a) A placing pole to a jump:

With a trot approach the pole would be at between 8ft (2.4m) and 9ft (2.7m).

With a canter approach the distance would be at least 9ft (2.7m). This would be for riders and horses with a great deal of experience – it would be less appropriate for novice riders. If using a canter pole with novice riders setting it at two canter strides away from the fence (approx. 30-33 ft [approx 9-10 m] is safer).

(b) For a bounce:

A bounce from trot would be 9–10 ft (2.7–3m).

From canter the bounce would be 10–12ft (3–3.6m).

(c) For a one non-jumping stride combination:

With a trot approach the distance would be about 18ft (5.4m).

With a canter approach the distance would be between 21ft (6.3m) and 24ft (7.2m).

(d) For a two non-jumping stride combination:

With a trot approach the distance would be about 28ft (8.4m).

With a canter approach the distance would be between 30ft (9m) and 33ft (9.9m).

Q. Explain what is meant by a related distance and how would you set it up when teaching. Give examples of distances you would use for three and four strides.

A. A related distance is two jumps, placed in such a way that when jumped one after the other there is a set number of strides in canter between the two jumps.

A three-stride related distance would be between 42ft (12.6m) and 48ft (14.4m).

A four-stride related distance would be between 51ft (15.3m) and 57ft (17.1m).

When teaching, develop the rider's feel for a good rhythm in canter and then start with two poles on the ground and help the rider to be able to feel or count the number of strides between poles. Gradually introduce jumps, keeping the first fence smaller while building up the second fence so that the rider finds it easy to jump in to the related distance with confidence and then build their ability to ride the related strides in a good flowing rhythm.

Q. Moving show jumps can be done with efficiency. Explain how you would carry wings and poles and how four or five fences can be erected quickly for a lesson, using one helper.

A. Keep all cups in a bucket so that they are safe and can be easily carried about and not lost on the floor.

Move heavy wings between two of you. Ideally, use light plastic equipment that is easily moved by one person.

Place poles at the site of where you want the jump and let your helper then bring the wings or blocks.

Choose a simple plan that keeps all the jumps in one area so that moving fences a long way is not time consuming.

If building a grid or combination, place it nearest the jump store, with the plain single jump furthest away.

Q. Is it important for once-a-week riders to have the same instructor each time?

A. The advantages would be that the riders would have confidence in the instructor with whom they are familiar. There is likely to be better continuity if the instructor knows the pupils and can relate to their weekly progress. The pupils are more likely to confide their hopes and fears to someone they know well.

The advantages of having a different instructor would be that a fresh eye can bring a new input or appraisal of the riders and different relevant exercises.

Q. Do you keep records of progress of riders? Are tests for clients appropriate?

A. It is wise to keep some records of progress for riders because then it is easier to follow through with progressive work especially if different instructors are taking the lessons. Rider registration forms must be updated regularly.

Tests for riders can provide a challenge and incentive to progress for riders. It can give them a bench mark of where they are in their riding compared to e.g. a year ago.

Q. How important is it to be aware of basic faults such as poor mounting and incorrect altering of stirrups, that creep in, despite initial correct teaching? Give other examples.

A. It is vital that a correct procedure is maintained and adhered to in all basic management and riding of the horse or eventually a casual fault will cause an accident.

Other examples: taking a coat off when mounted without either having someone hold the horse or being sure that you keep hold of the reins; lining up too close to other horses and allowing them to touch noses casually or swing their quarters towards each other; crowding horses together when leaving the arena (mounted or unmounted)

Q. You are planning an 'own a pony week'. What will you include and how will you ensure safety in the various tasks and riding activities?

A. One child per pony, each child to be monitored and supported by one instructor either directly if less competent or through a more competent member of the group who has experience of the type of day.

Include catching ponies (controlled and organised) grooming, tacking up, riding, untacking, cleaning tack, care of ponies after work. Some theory of pony care, some fun activity, mounted or unmounted, games or treasure hunt.

At all times the children must be supervised and the activities must be structured to ensure safety and organised fun.

Q. What are the Progressive Riding Tests? Can they benefit the riding school as well as clients?

A. Progressive Riding Tests are tests set by the BHS for adults and juniors to give them a gauge of their riding and stable management ability.

There are six tests for adults and five for juniors and these can be split into riding and stable management. Riders can be assessed for individual sections when they are ready.

They can benefit the riding school by giving the school the chance to run courses and training aimed towards achieving the tests.

If all six adult tests are passed a rider can have direct access to the BHS Stage 2 exam.

Q. In a riding school where hacking includes some road work, would you encourage and train clients for the BHS Riding and Road Safety Test? What is involved?

A. The Riding and Road Safety Test is a useful addition to the training and knowledge of any rider who will ride on the public highway.

The test involves a comprehensive multiple-choice question paper on all aspects of road safety as delivered by the Highway Code, but with specific reference to horse riding. (All the relevant information can be found in The British Horse Society's booklet, Riding and Roadcraft, published by Kenilworth Press.) There is also a ridden section on a simulated road, involving tests and hazards, and a further section which is assessed on a route set on a public highway.

Q. When a client asks you a question that you cannot answer, what do you do?

A. Ask a senior member of the establishment or your own instructor, or tell the person that you don't know the answer but will find out and come back to them on it.

Q. Discuss some qualities of a good instructor/coach.

A. Patience

Good knowledge and ability to put that across

Stamina

Good clear voice

Sense of humour

Enthusiasm

Confidence

Authority

Awareness

Fairness

Q. Why is feedback an important part of teaching?

A. Your pupils learn from the feedback that you give them.

They should be able to build on positive feedback.

It should give them a clear picture of where their strengths and weaknesses are and how to address them.

It allows for two-way communication between you and your pupil.

Q. What do you understand by the term 'motivation'?

A. Motivation is the 'drive' or incentive to want to do better.

Q. Discuss some ways you could motivate: (a) children, (b) adults, during a riding lesson.

A. Giving them a challenge to be better than each other often motivates children.

Giving them a specific aim, which they can all try to achieve, often motivates children (e.g. Who can get closest to the cone in the corner? Who can touch the cone from their pony?).

Adults may be motivated by a more individual aim (e.g. today we are aiming to canter for the first time).

Seeing someone else achieve the goal they are aiming for may motivate adults.

Q. How would you motivate riders who were not keen to ride?

A. Find out why they are not keen to ride. It may not be sensible to try to encourage them to ride if they really do not want to.

Riding is a sport that needs a degree of self-motivation.

Handling the horse and feeling more confident around him before riding him may encourage them.

It can help if they have ridden a mechanical horse, when they need have no fear of not being in control.

Q. What teaching methods could you adopt to motivate a class of teenage riders who have had to ride in the indoor school for several weeks due to bad weather?

A. Ask each rider to choose an exercise to explain to the rest of the class, and then the class ride it.

Make a mini competition on the best rider position, making them give themselves a mark out of ten (one being low and ten being high).

Do the same without stirrups and encourage them to improve on their own mark.

Do similar exercises but ask them to mark each other.

Q. What do you understand by 'goal setting' when teaching riders?

A. Goal setting is setting aims for riders which are achievable either in the sessional, short or long term. The goal must be measurable and realistic to the specific pupil.

A sessional goal might be to learn about diagonals in trot this week, a short goal may be to be able to recognise and change diagonal efficiently and a long-term goal may be to be able to feel which diagonal you are on on every horse you ride.

Q. Discuss the types of goal you could set for different riders (e.g. individual lessons in dressage or jumping, lead-rein lessons, class lessons, lunge lessons and stable management lessons).

A. The answer to this question could fill a small book in its own right. However, to help you answer this constructively in the exam, we will consider some options.

With all lessons the following criteria will help you to set the appropriate goals:

In a private lesson, consider the age and ability of the rider, how often they ride – so how fit they might be.

Ask them what they would like to do (in case they have a burning desire about something).

Consider the length of time you have to teach.

Consider the facilities you have. The goal for a novice child in a safe indoor school will be very different to the goal for that same child outside in a large field.

Consider the weather conditions. A lesson in walk on a hot day may be appropriate, whereas on a cold frosty day it would not.

Agree the goal with the rider. If the rider does not want to canter, that should not be your goal!

In a class lesson, there are other considerations such as whether all riders are of the same or similar ability, and, if you are likely to choose a jumping goal, whether all riders are mounted on horses/ponies that jump.

Lead-rein lessons are generally easier to set clear goals for, because you, as the leader, have total control over the pace of the horse/pony, which allows you to limit any problems that might arise.

Similarly, lunge lessons would usually be directed at some form of rider position improvement.

Stable-management lessons should be directed towards something that interests the pupil and helps them to be a more independent rider.

Listed below are one or two typical goals for each type of lesson.

Private dressage lesson. Improve awareness of rhythm in all three paces. Improve the basic transitions from one pace to another.

Private jumping lesson. Improve basic position using several fences in a simple grid. Improve the rider's ability to canter into a jump.

Lead-rein lesson. Improve the rider's confidence in going from rising trot to sitting to make a downward transition. Basic work without stirrups.

Class lesson. Improve the riding of turns and circles. Improve the knowledge of methods of changing the rein.

Lunge lesson. Improve the feel for the horse by identifying when the hind legs touch the ground. Improve the use of diagonals in trot.

Stable management lessons. Learning how to put on and fit tack.

Q. Consider each type of lesson and the type of goals you might set for an experienced rider and a more novice rider in the short and long-term situation.

A. The potential answers to this question are diverse and variable, and may be influenced by such things as the weather conditions, the confidence of the rider on 'that day', the frequency with which they ride, and other factors. The things to remember are that while planning and 'goal setting' are very important in any lesson, it is also vital that you teach 'what you see on the day' and do not stick rigidly to a plan or goal if that becomes unachievable due to an unforeseen reason.

- As a guide for an experienced rider in a class lesson:

    A **short-term goal** might be to work on the ability to slightly shorten and lengthen the horse's stride in trot, while working for a short period without stirrups to improve the rider's depth of position.

    A **long-term goal** might be to ride one specific horse to develop the range in all his paces, while linking the work to the development of lateral movements, which enhances the work further.

- For an experienced rider in an individual lesson:

  A **short-term goal** may be to understand the aids for turn on the forehand and to begin to be able to ride this movement.

  A **long-term goal** may be to have a greater understanding and feel for these movements and how they relate to the training of the horse and the feel for improving the paces.

- Choice of goals for novice riders would be much more aimed at consolidating the basic learning of things like:

  Basic correct position, balance and security.

  Basic understanding of the aids, how to apply them and how to develop coordination.

  Basic ability to ride transitions (simple transitions between each pace).

  Ability to ride simple turns and circles and to understand the basic principles of rhythm, suppleness, speed of the pace, contact between hand and leg, forwardness and balance.

  Remember that for novice and experienced riders there are a range of experiences which can be included to develop their versatility and enjoyment as riders – for example, working in the school, in the fields, out hacking in the countryside, polework, jumping, independent riding (alone and in company). All these experiences could be built into any goal-setting programme.

Q. Imagine you are teaching a keen adult rider who has fallen off while jumping in a previous lesson and has lost their nerve. How would you proceed with your lesson/s to increase the rider's confidence?

A. Find out how they feel about the fall (whether they accept it was 'one of those things'/an occupational hazard, or are very negative about the circumstances of the fall).

Consider mounting them on a different horse on which they feel happy.

Go back to basic work in jumping position and over poles without any thought of jumping.

Wait until the rider actually wants to jump again before introducing a fence.

Work them in a group where other riders are addressing similar issues, so that the rider does not feel isolated in their own experience.

Q. If you are teaching a beginner rider who is not making much progress, what could you suggest to help to improve them?

A. Find out how they feel about their progress; it may not bother them that they are not making faster progress and so they are not trying particularly hard.

Try to put them in a group where there are other riders of a similar standard so that may help to motivate them to progress as the others do.

Perhaps change the instructor or the horse they ride.

Perhaps suggest a lunge lesson or private lesson.

Q. What do you understand by the terms 'positive thinking' and 'negative thinking'?

A. People who think positively tend to see the bright side of things; they tend to be optimistic in their thinking and this can often affect their progress. They believe they are good and will tend to do better than negative thinkers, who are inclined to put themselves down and be pessimistic about their progress.

Q. How can positive thinking while (a) teaching and (b) riding affect your performance? Conversely, how can negative thinking affect a rider's and teacher's performance?

A. Consider this carefully and study some literature on sports psychology in the realm of positive/negative thinking. Consider your own attitude as both a rider and when teaching or being taught.

Q. How could you help the rider who has to ride a horse that no one else wants to?

A. Have a policy in the school that everyone rides every horse (according to their ability).

Encourage riders to see it is a positive advantage to develop their experience when riding something that is not liked.

Tell the rider that next week they can ride a horse of their choice.

Q. **Can you give some reasons that may negatively affect a rider's performance?**

A. Tiredness, illness.

Emotional problems (e.g. row with parent or boy/girlfriend).

Other worries (e.g. exams at school/college, money worries).

Fear of a past experience being repeated.

Q. **Why do you think it is important to review a rider's performance at regular intervals?**

A. To consider progress and make sure that the rider is progressing at an acceptable rate for them, taking all circumstances into consideration (e.g. how often they ride).

To ensure that the rider is happy with the agreed goals.

To reconsider the goals if some have been achieved and more need to be set.

Q. **Clients like to feel valued. Why is this important and how can you ensure they do?**

A. Everyone likes to feel valued, it is human nature.

Treat them as an individual (not as a number).

Know their name and speak to them personally whenever you can even if they are not one of your particular clients.

Involve them personally in decisions which affect them (goals, worries, progress).

Q. How can you encourage your clients to keep returning for lessons? What mechanism does the BHS provide to encourage riders to return for lessons?

A. Treat them as individuals.

Be interested in their progress.

Work out a personal plan for their development and needs.

Run classes and training days that appeal to what they want.

Have a club or loan horse system in your school which they can feel a part of.

The BHS runs the Progressive Riding Tests which your school can utilise in many ways to stimulate learning, enthusiasm for lessons and training.

A BHS approved establishment should offer a well-run centre in which a rider can develop their passion for their sport of riding.

Q. What is meant by the term 'duty of care'?

A. It is the adult's responsibility when in charge of children or vulnerable adults, to provide a safe environment for them in whatever activity they are involved.

The adult has a duty to provide as safe a situation as is possible for the welfare and well-being of any child.

Q. What age group is 'legally' classified as a 'child'?

A. Individuals up to the age of eighteen.

Q. Why is it important for riding instructors and coaches to have awareness of child protection issues?

A. Riding is a very physical sport and there are instances when a riding instructor may make contact with a child (e.g. legging up the rider, going to a rider who has fallen off and is distressed).

The position of the instructor in relation to helping a child must never be in question.

The relationship between child and teacher must always be of unquestionable integrity.

Q. What do you understand by 'good practice'? Give some examples of good practice when working with children.

A. Good practice is carrying forward training that is within the capability of the pupil(s) following a clear pathway of progress with clear explanation of work and much opportunity for the pupil to feed back on satisfactory progress.

Good practice with children would include clear but short explanation of work without overloading or confusing the child with information.

Short sessions of work so that the child is not bored or over-tired by the lesson.

Opportunity for two-way communication with the child to monitor progress and feedback.

Q. What sort of things should be avoided as poor practice?

A. Overwork so that the child is tired or disillusioned.

Over-criticism so that the child feels inadequate and disappointed.

Q. What special considerations or care must be taken when teaching children as opposed to adults?

A. Children may not be brave enough to tell you that they are cold, wet or tired.

Children may not be brave enough to tell you that they are afraid to do something or that they do not understand.

Q. Do you think it is a good idea to allow parents to become involved in their children's lessons?

A. It can be helpful if it is well controlled and the parents do not interfere (e.g. small child being led by parent although the instructor controls the lesson).

It can be detrimental if the parent takes over the lesson or the parent is saying one thing and the instructor another.

Q. What sort of problems could be caused by parents who are over- anxious about their child's safety?

A. They make the child more insecure and doubting of their own ability.

They cause disruption for other members of the class.

They affect the attitude of other parents.

Q. How would you deal with parents who are too pushy or over ambitious?

A. Firmly! Talk to them privately about the standards that the establishment sets and explain that you as the professional instructor rely on them to trust your ability and leave you to make the choices about what their child does or does not do in a lesson.

Q. What sort of things might cause you to have concerns about the welfare of a child in your ride?

A. A change in behaviour from normal (child normally outgoing becomes withdrawn or tearful).

Inconsistent behaviour or attendance from a normally consistent child.

Signs of physical abuse such as unexplained bruising on arms or face.

Q. What would you do/whom would you contact if you had concerns about the welfare of a child in your ride?

A. Go and discuss the issue with a senior member of staff or the Club Welfare Officer (CWO).

Q. What would you do if one of the children in your ride or on the yard was being bullied or verbally abused by the other children?

A. If you see it actually happening then you must deal with the culprit and in doing so you must involve the parents of that child and if necessary ban the child from attending lessons in future until the behaviour is guaranteed to change.

If you only suspect it is happening, then you must try to get the confidence of the child being bullied or a friend who will give you the necessary evidence to tackle the issue.

You cannot act on hearsay and in every situation must deal very carefully with the circumstances.

Q. Where can you get information and advice on teaching people with disabilities?

A. Through the Riding for the Disabled Association. There is a national office and then most regions have a local group who would be able to offer local knowledge and assistance.

Q. How is it possible to protect children and vulnerable adults?

A. It is possible to safeguard by adopting the BEF Child Protection Policy and BHS Instructors Register and Code of Conduct. There are also helpful tools such as Risk Assessment, safe recruitment procedures, staff training and accurate record keeping. All instructors should work using good practice procedures at all times.

Q. Where can you get further information from?

A. NSPCC, CPSU and BEF member body lead welfare officers which can be found by contacting the BEF.

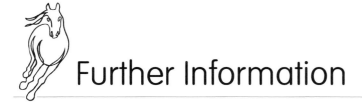

Further Information

Useful contacts

Child Protection in Sport Unit (CPSU)
0116 234 7278
www.cpsu.org.uk

NSPCC helpline
0808 800 5000
www.nspcc.org.uk

British Equestrian Federation
02476 698871
www.bef.co.uk

The British Horse Society
02476 840500
www.bhs.org.uk

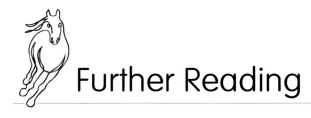

Further Reading

The following books and booklets can all be obtained from the BHS Bookshop.

The BHS Complete Manual of Horse and Stable Management

The BHS Veterinary Manual Second Edition

The BHS Complete Manual of Equitation

The BHS Manual for Coaching and Teaching Riding

The BHS Complete Training Manual for Stage 1

The BHS Complete Training Manual for Stage 2

The BHS Complete Training Manual for Stage 3

**The BHS Training
Manual for Progres-
sive Riding Tests 1-6**

**The BHS Stage 1
Workbook**

**The BHS Stage 2
Workbook**

**The BHS Riding and
Roadcraft 12th Edition**

**Learn to Ride with the
British Horse Society**

BHS TREC

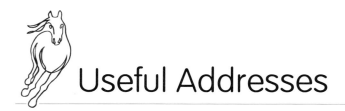

Useful Addresses

The British Horse Society
Abbey Park
Kenilworth
Warwickshire
CV8 2XZ
tel: 02476 840500
fax: 02476 840501
website: www.bhs.org.uk
email: enquiry@bhs.org.uk

BHS Bookshop
(address as left)
tel: 02476 840540
website: www.britishhorse.com

BHS Standards Directorate

BHS Examinations Department
(address as above)
tel: 02476 840508
email: exams@bhs.org.uk

BHS Training Department
(address as above)
tel: 02476 840510
email: training@bhs.org.uk

BHS Riding Schools/Approvals
Department
(address as above)
tel: 02476 840509
email: Riding.Schools@bhs.org.uk

BHS Safety Department
(address as above)
tel: 02476 840516
email: safety@bhs.org.uk

Qualification Structure

Scottish Vocational Qualifications & Work Based Diplomas	UKCC Endorsed Qualifications	Equestrian Tourism Qualifications	BHS Horse Knowledge and Care Exams	BHS Riding Exams	BHS Coaching and Teaching Exams	BHS Qualifications
						Fellowship of the BHS
			BHS Stable Managers Certificate	BHS Senior Equitation Certificate	BHS Senior Coaching Certificate	BHS Instructors Certificate
		Centre Manager	Stage 4 Horse Knowledge and Care	Stage 4 Riding	BHS Intermediate Teaching Test	BHS Intermediate Instructors Certificate (Equine Coach)
SVQs & Work Based Diplomas Horse Care & Management (Level 3)	Certificate in Coaching UKCC endorsed EQL Level 3 (Equine) EQL Level 3 Award in the Principles of Coaching Sport	Ride Leader	Stage 3 EQL Level 3 Diploma in BHS Horse Knowledge and Care EQL Level 3 Certificate in Horse Care EQL Level 3 Award in the Principles of Horse Care	Stage 3 EQL Level 3 Diploma in BHS Riding Horses EQL Level 3 Certificate in Riding Horses on the Flat	EQL Level 3 Certificate in BHS Preliminary Teaching of Horse Riding	BHS Assistant Instructors Certificate (Equine Coach)
SVQs & Work Based Diplomas Horse Care (Level 2)	Certificate in Coaching UKCC endorsed EQL Level 2 (Equine) EQL Level 2 Award in the Principles of Coaching Sport	Assistant Ride Leader	Stage 2 EQL Level 2 Diploma in BHS Horse Knowledge and Care EQL Level 2 Certificate in Horse Care EQL Level 2 Award in the Principles of Horse Care	Stage 2 EQL Level 2 Diploma in BHS Riding Horses EQL Level 2 Certificate in Riding Horses on the Flat Riding & Road Safety EQL Level 2 in BHS Riding Horses Safely on the Public Highway		
SVQs & Work Based Diplomas Horse Care (Level 1)	Certificate in Coaching UKCC endorsed EQL Level 1 Award in the Principles of Coaching Sport		Stage 1 EQL Level 1 Certificate in BHS Horse Knowledge and Care	Stage 1 EQL Level 1 Certificate in BHS Riding Horses		

The British Horse Society

EQL
Equestrian Qualifications GB Limited